A LONG OVERDUE

THANK YOU

PAYING HOMAGE

TO

TO FOUNDATIONAL

BLACK

AMERICANS

AND OTHER UNSUNG HEROES HERE AND ABROAD

CAROLYN JO VINING

THANK YOU

Printed in the United States of America

ISBN: 978-0-578-33851-4

Carolyn Jo Vining

Contents

DEDICATION

❧

Lest never Forget

The triumphant but also grave sacrifices of those that
came before us.

This is dedicated to

THE ANCESTORS

"My Ancestors,

Foundational Black American blood runs all through this here American Soil.

For they have already overpaid for my rights to this land."

CJV

To be disconnected
from your own
Ancestors is to be
disconnected from
your own soul

Chapter

1

Who are we Really?

❦

What did every black grandmother always say back in the day?

"You got some Indian in you."

Our claim to this land

Before I even get started, I want to make sure this point is crystal clear:

To ALL my people of color and people in the struggle WORLDWIDE, I AM SO PROUD OF YOU!

I should hope that emotion is reciprocated.

People of color and poor people have been subjugated and exploited worldwide. This book is an ODE, so to speak, paying long overdue homage to Foundational Black Americans and their triumphant struggle in the good old USA.

In history class in school, they teach us that Foundational Black Americans are all from Africa, this is not true.

We are so much more!

We are Moors.

We are Maroons.

We are Cowboys,

We are Indians (Natives).

We are all these things.

We are AMERICAN.

I was going to dedicate this book to my father, a Foundational Black American. He served his country in the Vietnam war but was poisoned by Agent Orange, to be left for dead back in his home country.

Oh yes, my people have paid the ultimate price to build this nation, our nation everyone enjoys.

We paid with our blood, our lives, our children, our souls, our spirits, our families, our bodies, our sweat, our tears, our cries, OUR PAIN paved these roads in America the great.

I also thought about dedicating this book to my grandmother, my dad's mother and a foundational Black American. Her grandmother was an actual prisoner of war (slave).

My grandmother was born into poor sharecropping in Little Rock, Arkansas. Because we all know after slavery was "over," white people got compensated and black people got zero. She ran away to California as a teenager with my father in tow.

Well, let me tell you about my grandmother!

She worked hard and did whatever she could to survive.

She was the pillar of the family, the epitome of a strong black woman. At her death, she owned four properties in Los Angeles worth over a million dollars today.

A true American queen.

Making something out of nothing.

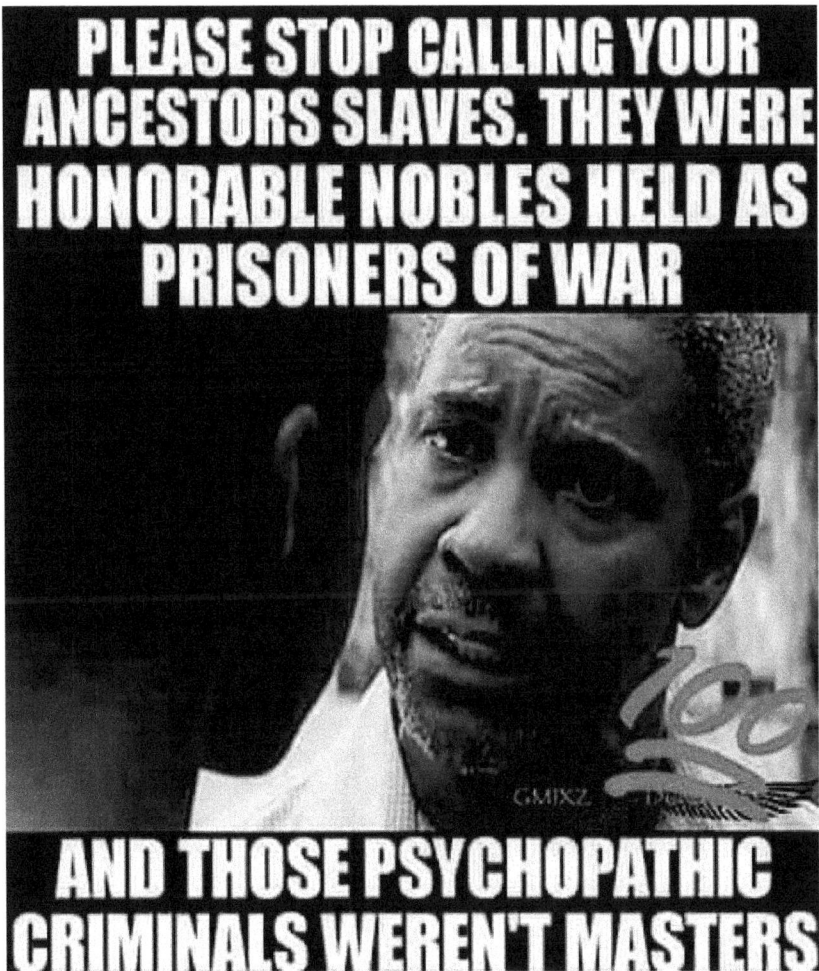

PLEASE STOP CALLING YOUR ANCESTORS SLAVES. THEY WERE HONORABLE NOBLES HELD AS PRISONERS OF WAR

AND THOSE PSYCHOPATHIC CRIMINALS WEREN'T MASTERS

But my heart tells me to dedicate this book to my ancestors who came in chains on the bottom of a slave ship and to the majority of us who were already here—those held captive and made to work over 200 years **for free** to build this country.

All the while being terrorized, dehumanized, brutalized, raped, sodomized, and maimed. With kids sold, families torn apart, hunted down like dogs by slave catchers just for trying to be free, whipped regularly, psychologically traumatized, made to bid on own family members, hung from trees, locked away in farms made to breed like animals, made to have babies you would never get to hold, black babies used as alligator bait, whole black communities and towns attacked and burned down to the ground, branded like cattle, burned alive and hung for entertainment, the law allowing us to be hunted and tracked by dogs (fugitive slave act), If any other race would even try to help us, they were threatened with death.

Foundational Black Americans built the United States into the world power it is today with free labor, torture, and blood.

"Give me the free labor of one Black person for one year I would be a rich man. Give me the free labor of a dozen Black people for 10 years, I would be a very rich man. Give me the free labor of millions of Black people for 250 years, I would be America."
~ Ralph Wiley/Sports Journalist

Everyone owes my ancestors a long overdue Thank you.

Their perseverance and superhuman abilities to survive and overcome should never be forgotten.

Now, I want to address the point I just made that most of us were already here in America, as the majority of us are indigenous Black Americans.

If you grew up in a black household in America -one of your elders would always say, "you got some Indian in you."

To lie and say we are all from Africa and came on a slave ship was just another way to disenfranchise us so we would not lay any claim to this land- our land, as a Foundational Black American.

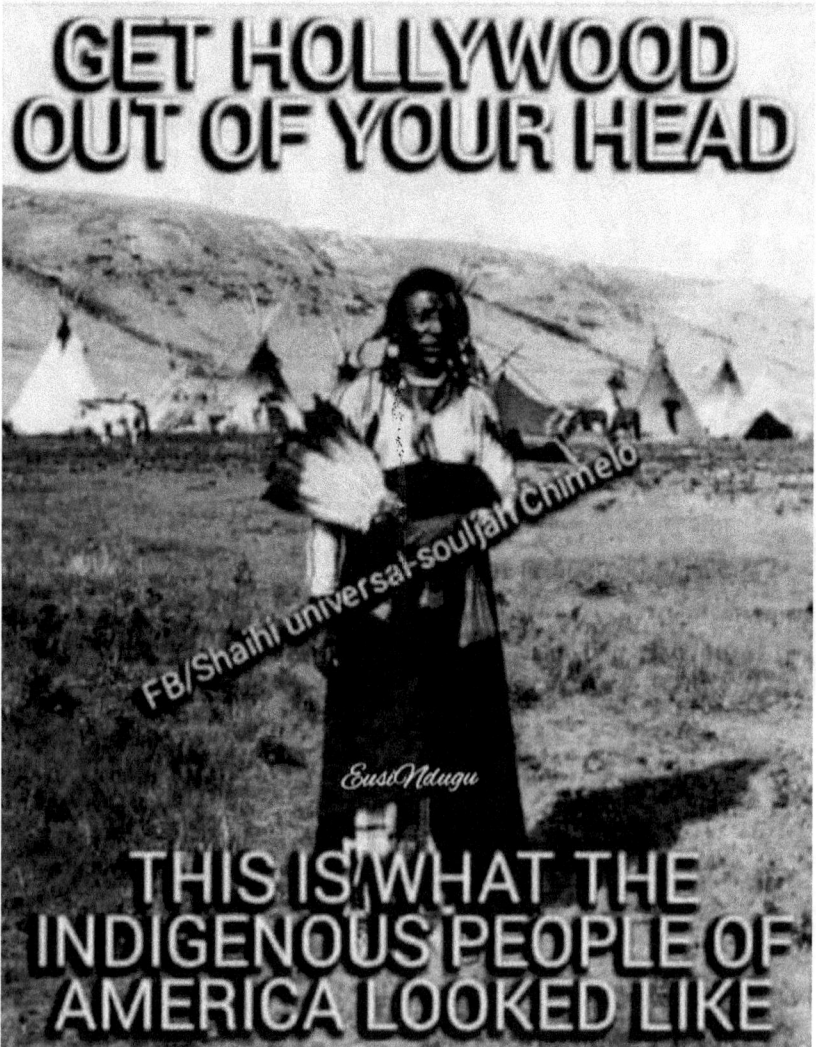

1850 PORTRAIT OF A CHOCTAW INDIAN IN NEW ORLEANS BY ALFRED BOISSEAU

CHIEF WARHORSE, CHAHTA NEW ORLEANS

NEW ORLEANS CHOCTAW

NEGROES TALKING ABOUT "LET'S GET BACK TO AFRIKAN CONSCIOUSNESS!!", "LET'S GET BACK TO AFRIKAN SPIRITUALITY!!", BUT THEIR MOMMA, DADDY, GRANDPA, GRANDMA, GREAT GRANDMA (x10) NEVER SAID THEY WERE AFRICANS. THE ONLY PEOPLE THAT SAID AMERICAN NEGROES WERE "STOLEN AFRICANS" IS THE EDUCATION GIVEN TO THEM BY THE WHITE ESTABLISHMENT'S CATHOLIC & PUBLIC SCHOOL SYSTEM. WHAT PAN-AFRICAN NEGROES REALLY MEAN IS LET'S KEEP WHITE SUPREMACY'S AFRICANIZED LIES IN PLACE.

+JOHNNIE ABORIGINE

@JOHNNIEABORIGINE

1900

EMMA CURRY PITCHLYNN MISSISSIPPI CHOCTAW INDIAN

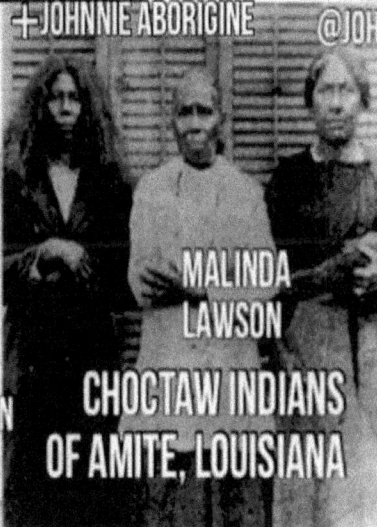

MALINDA LAWSON

CHOCTAW INDIANS OF AMITE, LOUISIANA

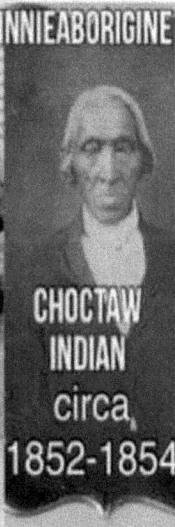

CHOCTAW INDIAN circa 1852-1854

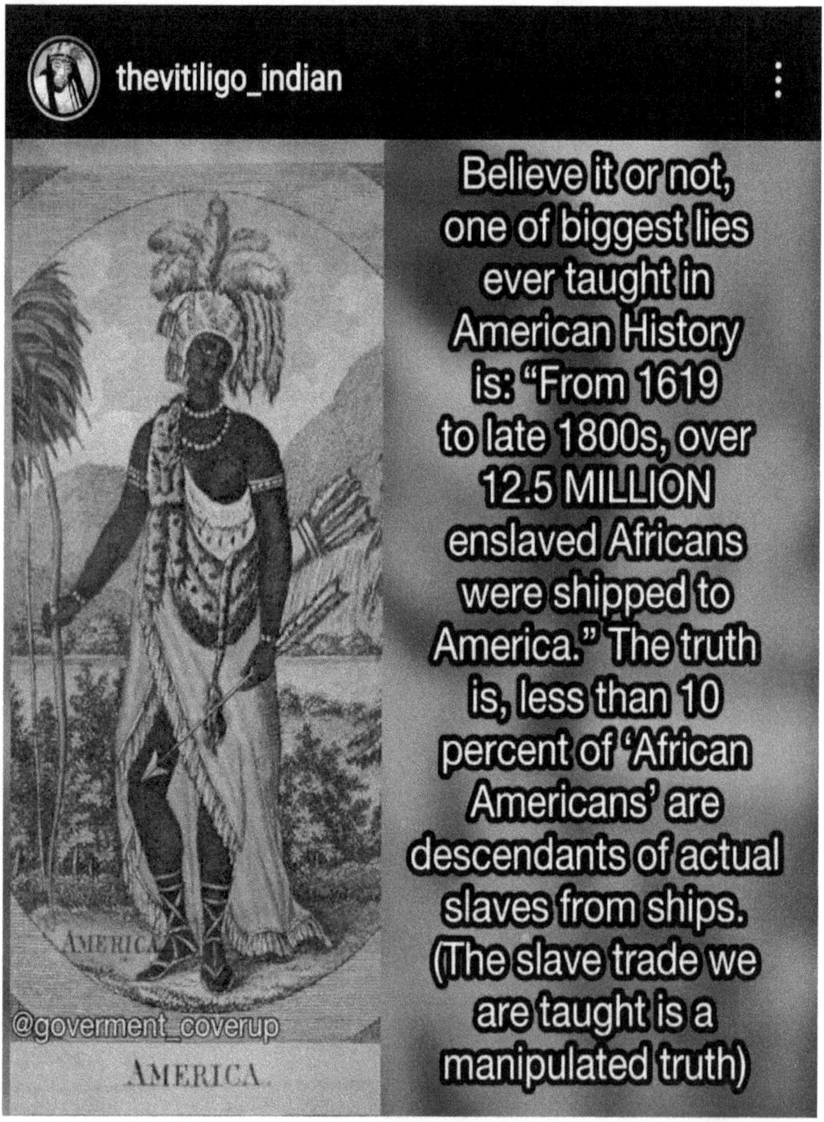

thevitiligo_indian

Believe it or not, one of biggest lies ever taught in American History is: "From 1619 to late 1800s, over 12.5 MILLION enslaved Africans were shipped to America." The truth is, less than 10 percent of 'African Americans' are descendants of actual slaves from ships. (The slave trade we are taught is a manipulated truth)

@goverment_coverup

AMERICA.

The Story of
The Negro:
The Rise of the Race from
Slavery
(Vol. 1)

Booker T. Washington

FB/IG Autochthons of America

"I venture to say that the amount of Indian blood in the American Negro is very much larger than anyone who has not investigated the subject would be inclined to believe."
➺➺➺page 131
-Booker T Washingtor

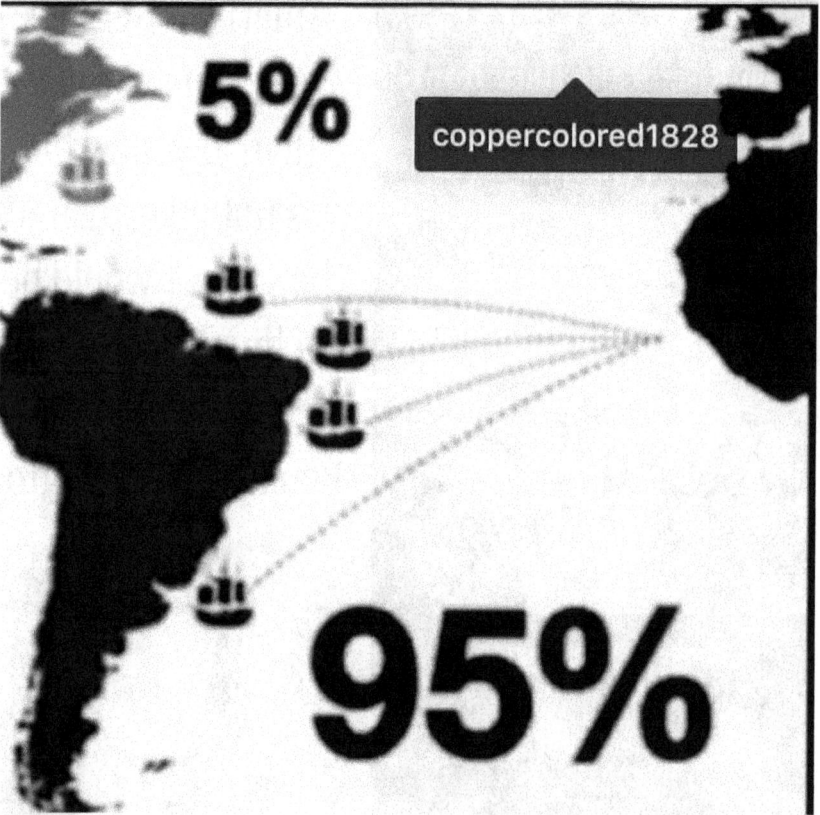

AMERICAN

Q. What is the third race, and what are its characteristics?

569. The American or Indian Race, found only in America, is of a deep copper color; straight, black hair, high cheek bones; eyes black and sunken, large faces, and robust bodies.

This race comprises all the American Indians, except the Esquimaux, who belong to the Asiatic race.

tasha_xi ...

Virginia passed two acts in 1682 that combined Native Americans and Africans into one category as negroes and other slaves.

Lamond BigBoy Finch
2 HOURS AGO

♥ **Kimoni Bravehorse**

"Before the White people came over to America, it had many tribes of people in it. Some of these tribes still remain in the United States, and in the countries north of it, and in South America. These form what are called the American race. They have a copper-colored skin—long, black hair—small, dark eyes—and very thick lips, and broad noses." (Beecher-Stowe, 1833).

Africa   Asia   Europe   America

But in all honesty, it doesn't matter if we were already here or came on a ship- my ancestors have given more to America than anyone else, and this is my homage to them.

I am a Foundational Black American.

This term was coined by the great filmmaker, historian, and teacher Tariq Nasheed.

If you go to my website, I will have more information about him and the Foundational Black American Flag. I will also put up a link for you to order one.

We are not slaves or never were slaves. We were made into slaves. It took two generations (over 60 years) before we even began to be broken enough and FORCED INTO slavery, thus becoming prisoners of war for hundreds of years. There were many, many uprisings of us trying to be free.

We were prisoners of war, nothing more, nothing less.

BLACK PEOPLE RESISTED

They resisted the practice of slavery and the trade in slaves from its inception in the United States in the early 1600s to its end in the middle 1800s.

They resisted it on the ships from Africa.

They resisted it in the fields and in the big house; they resisted by organized rebellion; and they resisted by direct, spontaneous acts of courage.

For their freedom, they killed and were killed. They poisoned and committed infanticide and suicide. They always ran away. And some master was always hunting for them.

Their will set against the master's will, they fought, fought back, and died. They also survived. They took the lash and the burn. They lost but they won.

By the strength of their determination, led by the North Star and set aboard the box cars of the Underground Railroad –by their resistance– slaves won in the cause of Human freedom.

The Decolonial Atlas is with **Tanya E Duarte**.

Nov 17, 2020 · 🌐

Today we remember Bet and Dinah, two teenage Black girls enslaved by the Van Rensselaer family in Albany, NY. On Nov 17, 1793, they lit a fire which burned down the homes of dozens of slave-owners, stoking fears of a slave uprising which likely hastened New York to abolish slavery. After confessing to the arson, Bet and Dinah were executed by the state.

Art: Eboni Hogan, instagram.com/the_wreckshop

Often native Foundational Black American heads were put on sticks lining the road to scare others from trying to revolt. This visual is from the Whitney plantation in Louisiana – I highly recommend a visit here – it is very moving and informative.

We come from fearless greatness and were prisoners of war for hundreds of years.

We are not AFRICAN Americans; we do not have the same culture.

If you dropped me (or, for that matter, any black person that I know of) off ANYWHERE in Africa right now, we would be lost!

We do not share the same languages, foods, or religions.

Our culture is uniquely different, as we were the only race forced to work for free for generations to build America.

My father was a Navy veteran who served in the Vietnam war.

My Grandmother's grandmother was a prisoner of war right here in the United States of America.

It does not get any more AMERICAN than that!

My great-great-grandmother helped to build this country for free!

And my father fought and risked his life for this very same country-MY COUNTRY!

So, the term I like to refer to people like myself is Foundational Black American.

I am a Foundational Black American, as my ancestors built this entire country from scratch for free!

So, this is paying homage to THEM!

We are Foundational Black Americans, and frankly, our unique culture is American culture.

OUR ANCESTORS BUILT THIS COUNTRY FROM SCRATCH, as there was nothing here before our free labor built it.

I am not disparaging or putting down anyone else for their culture. All people get to be proud of their own culture; this is just about OURS.

This book will be a brief and quick synopsis of what contributions you can thank Foundational Black Americans for.

And lastly, how we have been repaid for simply existing.

This is NOT a black vs. white thing; however, this is a right vs. wrong thing, the heinous acts (to put it mildly) that my ancestors ENDURED is the reason this country is as great as it is.

"JOHN HORSE" AND THE "BLACK SEMINOLES" LEAD THE BIGGEST SLAVE REBELLIOUS REVOLUTION IN U.S. HISTORY BUT YOU AND I WAS NEVER TAUGHT ABOUT HIM AND I WONDER WHY?

Contributions

from Foundational Black Americans

to the world

This section will only cover a small percentage of the overall contribution from my people to the world.

Thank You

Chattel Slavery and 246 years of free labor made America the greatest nation on Earth. Free labor from my ancestors poured billions of dollars into this economy, and the America we know now today couldn't have been as great without it.

When people from all over the world want to come to America for more opportunities and a better quality of life for themselves and their children, they can thank Foundational Black Americans for this dream and hope in America.

SOUTHERN HOSPITALITY

From the inception of this country, we, Foundational Black Americans, were the ones who cooked all the meals, cleaned the homes and asses of our captors and their children, shaved them, raised them, and even breastfed their children.

Even though I wasn't alive back then, I can clearly see how it was as I see how times are now, and although things change, some things have just mutated.

Not all white people owned or had slaves. We are referring to the wealthy white people, obviously. The ones who exist today have just replaced the slaves with indentured servants (mostly Hispanic these days).

Now I am by no means comparing people who were owned with no free will or choice by the threat of violence and the law, with someone who gets paid and can leave at any time. Still, know and be clear that it's just been changed up some, and still, these rich parasites feel their lives are more valuable than others.

My people, Foundational Black Americans, literally raised and breastfed this country into what it is today!

Foundational Black American Inventors/ inventions

This is a shortlist of what Foundational Black Americans have either invented, had a hand in inventing or improved upon the original invention of:

Remote control

Ice cream scoop

Automation of Elevator doors

Air conditioning unit

Almanac

Baby Stroller

Biscuit cutter

Blood plasma bag

Caller ID

Call waiting

Casket lowering device

Cell phone

Clothes dryer

Curtain rod

Doorknob

Doorstop

Dustpan

Fire extinguisher

Folding bed

Fountain pen

Gas Mask

Golf tee

GPS technology

Hairbrush

Helicopter

Ironing board

Lawn Mower

Lock

Lunch pail

Mailbox

Modern-day security systems

Mop

Peanut butter

Pencil sharpener

Performed first open-heart surgery

Potato chips

Refrigerated trucks

Rolling pin

Sanitary pad for women

Thermostat control

Touchtone phone

Traffic light

Tricycle

3D special effects

Not to mention the countless ideas stolen from us from Jack Daniels to KFC.

On behalf on my ancestors:

You're welcome!

This list is nothing less than remarkable, when for hundreds of years, we were not even allowed to learn to read.

Eyes gouged out and lye thrown in our eyes if we were to even get caught with a book, can you imagine?

The sacrifice of my ancestors – my heritage, here in my land in America, where my ancestor's bloodshed runs deeper here in this soil than anywhere else.

This is MY COUNTRY…

During slavery, the most forbidden weapon for slaves was knowledge.

And still…I RISE

Know her name: Jane Hinton was the scientist who made it possible for us to culture bacteria and test for antibiotic resistance. She was also one of the first African American women to gain the degree of Doctor of Veterinary Medicine

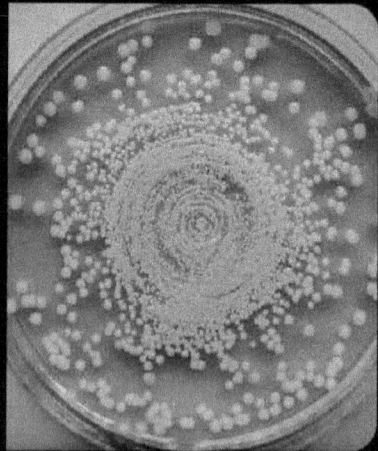

BMORE
NEWS.COM

This former slave was
making cars long before
nelvomedia Henry Ford

C. R. Patterson
1st African American-Owned
Automobile Manufacturer

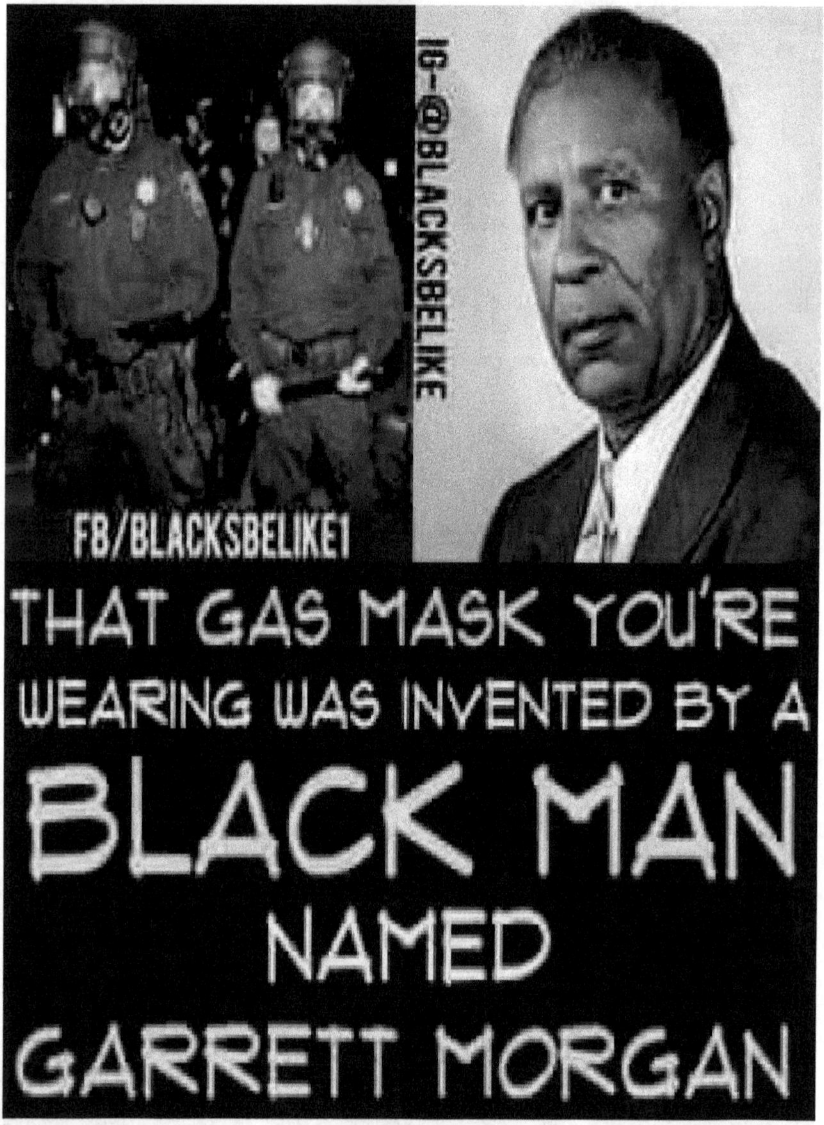
IG-@BLACKSBELIKE
FB/BLACKSBELIKE1
THAT GAS MASK YOU'RE
WEARING WAS INVENTED BY A
BLACK MAN
NAMED
GARRETT MORGAN

Ro Khanna ✓
@RoKhanna

In 1970s, Jerry Lawson created the first home gaming console that used cartridges instead of having games built directly into the hardware. His groundbreaking technology became the foundation for Atari, Nintendo, and Sega. #BlackHistoryMonth

Jerry Lawson, a self-taught engineer, gave us video game cartridges

In 1923, the company paid Morgan $40k ($620k today) for his patent and began to install his lights all over the country, ushering in the age of the 3-color traffic lights we know today.

@Blkpowermoves

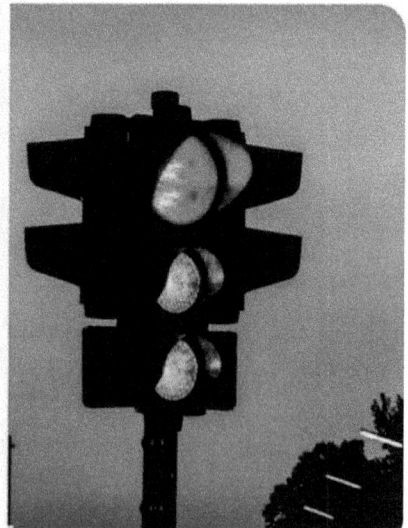

Did You Know? A Black Man Invented Flavored Icecream?!

Meet Augustus Jackson who was a White House chef from Philly who 1st manufactured ice cream by adding salt to ice while whipping the custard to control freezing. He also invented strawberry and mint chocolate icecream!

Dr. Patricia Era Bath, 1981. Inventor of the Laserphaco Probe, used worldwide in eye surgery to remove cataracts. Bath founded the American Institute for the Prevention of Blindness.

She restored sight to millions of people suffering from cataracts.

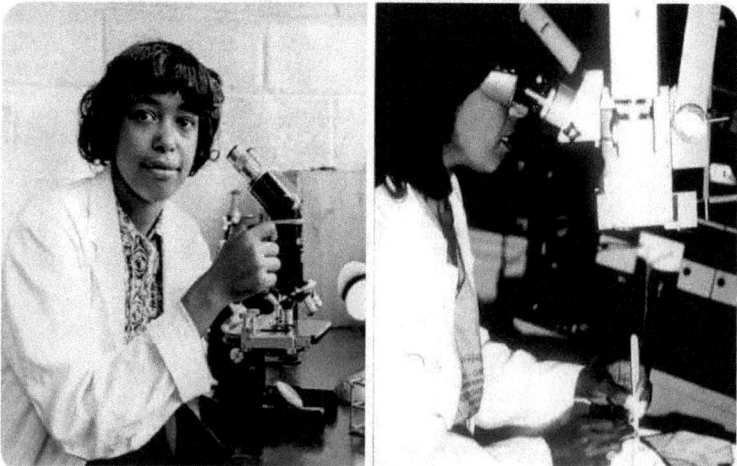

Foundational Black Americans are nothing short
of unstoppable, especially at our best…greatest
come up of all time

Chapter

2

"Putting in work"

❧

Civil Rights

When most people think of civil rights, the first thing that comes to mind is Martin Luther King and the most famous bus boycott.

Martin Luther King was the frontman and a famous world-renowned Foundational Black American Leader known around the world for fighting for equal rights for his people and all people of color around the world.

It's quite obvious this Foundational Black American man had a calling bigger than him.

In following his calling, he paid the highest price, and that was his life.

Although MLK was one of the most prolific, he was certainly not the only Foundational Black American to fight to change the status quo of two different classes of people living in the same country, a country claiming to but not having the same rights, freedoms, and opportunities for all.

The next most famous Foundational Black American to fight for equality and Freedom would be Malcolm X.

Malcolm X was a Human Rights Activist. Notice the term "Human Rights"? This encompasses all humans who are and were being left out of basic human rights – not just black people.

Although MLK and Malcolm X had very different ways of confronting and fighting injustices here in America, they both are Heros and deserve a long overdue Thank you!

Both of these men fought tirelessly and made it their life's mission to help others of all colors live a better quality life.

Malcolm X and Dr. **Martin Luther King Jr**. are two of the most iconic figures of the 20th century and the civil rights movement.

I Have a Dream...

A MAN WHO STANDS FOR NOTHING WILL FALL FOR ANYTHING.

MALCOLM X

Although these two Foundational Black American Men were modern-day Kings, the list goes on and on with how many of our people fought for change in this country for EVERYONE to benefit from.

Ella Baker was a not-so-famous name that was pivotal to the civil rights movement – she is known as the mother of Civil Rights.

Ella Jo Baker was born on December 13, 1903, in **Norfolk, Virginia**. Growing up in North Carolina, she developed a sense for social justice early on, due in part to her grandmother's stories about life under slavery.

After growing up in the horrors of the South at the beginning of the 19th century, she moved to New York in search of work and soon realized true equality was not to be found in the North either. This prompted her to help with the NAACP and later help found the Southern Christian Leadership Conference (SCLC).

Although both of these organizations were founded with great intentions, like most things that were started to benefit Foundational Black Americans – these entities have been corrupted and can no longer be trusted.

She worked with some of the most famous leaders of the 20th century. She also taught young children about civil rights and human rights.

Baker saw that economic justice was a key part of the struggle for freedom in general and for Black Americans in particular.

It was the Valiant efforts of Foundational Black Americans who fought and died for:

The 13th Amendment – Abolished Slavery

The **14th Amendment**- Granted citizenship to all persons "born or naturalized in the United States" and provided all citizens with Equal protections under the laws.

The **15th Amendment** – the right of citizens of the United States to vote shall not be denied or abridged on account of race, color or previous condition of servitude.

The Civil Rights Act of 1964- prohibits discrimination on the basis of race, color, religion, sex or national origin. The Act prohibited discrimination in public accommodations and federally funded programs. It also strengthened the enforcement of voting rights and the desegregation of schools

The Voting Rights Act of 1965- Prohibits racial discrimination when voting

Fair Housing Act of 1968- Prohibited discrimination concerning the sale, rental and financing of housing based on race, religion, national origin or sex.

The Bravery and resilience of Foundational Black Americans (and those that helped in the fight) is what has made America great for ALL PEOPLE.

All immigrants (especially those of color) should be thanking black Americans for the quality of life and freedoms they have here in America.

I am not going to make an exhaustive list of all our Civil Rights leaders, but on behalf of these three Black Americans, I want to say Your Welcome! As I believe they have not been recognized or Thanked Enough!

Just because laws had been hard fought for and passed does not mean everything suddenly became fair and all people were treated equally. Not by a long shot; we still had to fight!

The 1960s in the United States was a proverbial hot button for uprisings and boycotts to obtain the basic civil liberties we all in America enjoy today.

Not only did Foundational Black Americans boycott riding public transportation for over a year so we wouldn't have segregation on the bus, but there were also numerous other demonstrations demanding change.

1965- Selma to Montgomery Marches – Alabama – Marching for the right to vote.

Tennesee's tent cities were actually created because black tenants were evicted by their white landlords for registering to vote. This happened from 1959 to the 1970s; literally, black families were made homeless for standing up for their rights to vote.

1965- Watts Riots – Los Angeles over police brutality (it was horrible, I will get into this more on the section on the black panthers)

1966 – Omaha Riots – rioting over police brutality

1966 – 1966 Chicago Westside Riots – over police brutality

1966- Hough Riots Cleveland – tired over discrimination and unfair treatment

1966 – Marquette Park Housing March Chicago – protesting fair housing

1966 – Waukegan riot Illinois – tired of police brutality

1966 – Summerhill and Vine City Riots – Atlanta, Georgia – police brutality

1966 – Hunters Point social Uprising – San Francisco – police brutality

That list was just a very, very small snippet of all the work and fighting it took to get us where we are today.

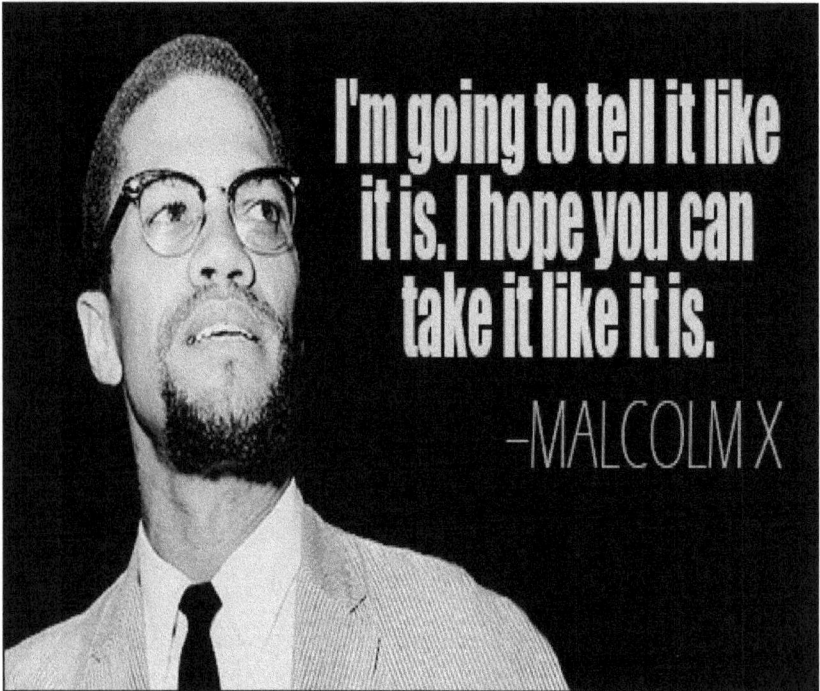

I'm going to tell it like it is. I hope you can take it like it is.

—MALCOLM X

After all these civil and equal rights were won and made into laws so everyone would have a chance at the "American Dream," lawmakers then focused on bringing as many other black people as they could here from other countries to America to drown us out and pit us against each other. If you're black but your people are from elsewhere, please do not let them use you to disrespect the very people who gave their lives for the opportunities you now enjoy in America.

NOONE has fought harder or paid a higher price for basic Freedoms here in America- but us!

On behalf of all my Foundational Black American Ancestors, YOU'RE WELCOME!

There is a reason we don't have foundational black
American leaders anymore as we did in the 1960's – we
were making too much noise and headway to progress, so
the powers that be shut it down.

A wise person once said, "the more things change, the more they stay the same."

I'd like to end this section with a personal story from my sister, who grew up in the 1960s and 1970s in Watts, California.

We were discussing the George Floyd situation, and this was her perspective:

Sis: I don't know why people are acting so surprised and crazy about what happened to George Floyd.

Me: What do you mean, sis? That was awful what they did to him

Sis: Yeah, it was, but that was nothing compared to what I had to live through and witness growing up in LA

Me: What do you mean?

Sis: I remember walking home from the bus or just walking to the store when I was growing up and seeing the police beat black men with their batons or even their fists all the time, almost on a daily basis

Me: Oh my God, that is horrible!

Sis: Yes, it was, And if anyone tried to help or intervene, they would just start beating us!

Carolyn! They had us trained to put our heads down and walk away fast or we knew we would be getting it next!

Me: Wow, so sorry you had to endure that!

Sis: yeah, and there was nowhere for us to turn. Not other police. Not the courts; nowhere and no one would help us!

Now, from just this story alone, can you imagine the Emotional scars incidents like these leave and have left on my people?

It is also stories like these that prompted the Black Panthers movement- we needed PROTECTION from somewhere...

The Black Panthers

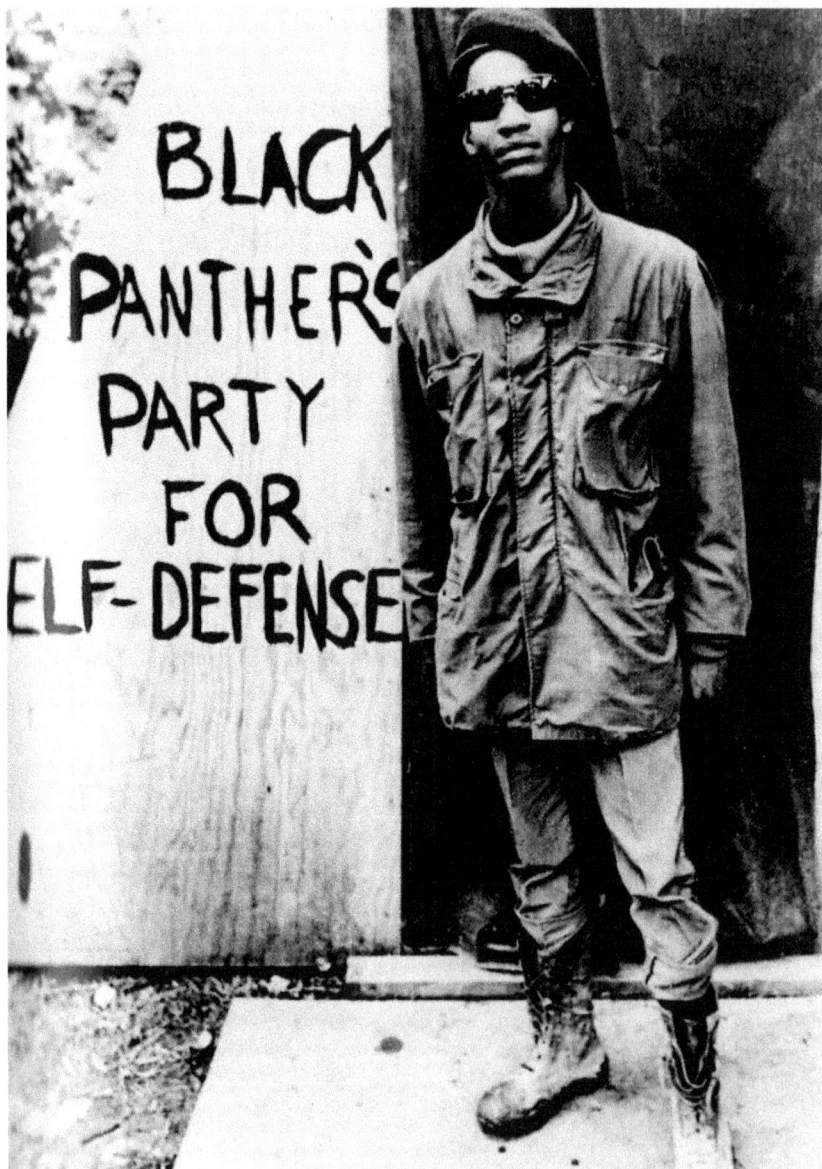

One of the main reasons for the Black Panthers forming was protection from Police Brutality.

They realized the police in our communities were not there to maintain order and safety, but they were actually enemies, brutalizing our people with protection under the law to do so.

The Black Panthers also recruited other marginalized groups for standing up for equality across the board, this is what scared the government the most and why they are not around to this day.

The Black Panthers were all about community, especially helping the poorest and the most oppressed.

They served thousands of meals daily while also operating free health clinics across the country for the poor and disenfranchised.

They also opened FREE QUALITY schools; they did what the government was refusing to do.

They started community programs nationwide.

The Black Panthers had women who were very vocal and active members, and at one time, over half of the entire party was female—which was unheard of at the time.

Here is a list of other notable accomplishments of the honorable Black Panther Party:

THE BLACK PANTHER PARTY REMAINS THE LARGEST REVOLUTIONARY BLACK AMERICAN ORGANIZATION EVER CREATED

While many organizations and movements have evolved after, some with similar names, the Black Panther Party remains the largest revolutionary group started by and for black Americans.

What first started as informal educational programs transformed into full-fledged schools with curriculums. The curriculums included traditional courses like English, math, and science, in addition to classes on black history and culture, and activities focused on class structure and the prevalence of institutional racism. These schools were called Liberation Schools, with the goals of providing students with education and training that were not accessible in "white schools." The most popular and successful one was the Oakland Community School.

THE BLACK PANTHER PARTY HAD A NEWSPAPER

Talking about telling your own story and taking control of the narrative, the Black Panther Intercommunal News Service served as the official voice of the Black Panther Party. It was published on April 25, 1967. The newspaper was distributed around the world to discuss BPP's philosophies and affairs. The paper was also a great source of revenue for the Party and helped to support the different branches and programs.

THE BLACK PANTHER PARTY WENT INTERNATIONAL

From its Oakland-based home, the Black Panther Party grew to chapters in 48 states in North America. Also, there were international support groups in Japan, France, Germany, Sweden, Algeria, South Africa, Zimbabwe, Uruguay, and many more.

THE BLACK PANTHER PARTY WELCOMED ALLIANCES WITH WHITE ACTIVISTS

The Black Panther Party welcomed alliances with white activists, such as the Students for a Democratic Society (SDS) and the Weathermen, because they believed that all revolutionaries who wanted to change systems of oppression in the United States should unite across racial lines.

THERE WAS A WHITE PANTHER PARTY THAT SUPPORTED THE GOALS OF THE BLACK PANTHER PARTY

The Black Panther Party was pro-black, not to be confused with anti-white. They welcomed white allies dedicated to eradicating systems of oppression for all. When asked what white people could do to support the Black Panther Party, Newton responded that they could form a **White Panther Party**. And thus, the far-left anti-racist white American group in support of BPP was founded in 1968 by Pun Plamondon, Leni Sinclair, and John Sinclair. They also had a similar ten-point program to support the goals of BPP.

THE BLACK PANTHER PARTY WAS IN SUPPORT OF ALL OPPRESSED GROUPS

Although the Party was founded to protect black Americans, the Black Panther Party was not trying to oppress anyone. In their 10-point program, BPP demanded rights and treatments for all people of color and all oppressed communities.

THE BLACK PANTHER PARTY'S FREE BREAKFAST FOR CHILDREN PROGRAM FORCED THE GOVERNMENT TO EXPAND ITS OWN SCHOOL FOOD PROGRAMS

The Black Panther Party offered many socialist programs. One program, in particular, was the free school breakfast program for children. This program was launched to "encourage the survival of black people and children." Although the program was one of the Party's most successful programs, it was eventually destroyed. However, the program had already received so much positive publicity that it pressured political leaders to feed children before school and resulted in the government expanding its school food programs.

THE BLACK PANTHERS CREATED MANY COMMUNITY PROGRAMS

In addition to the Free Breakfast for Children program and sickle cell anemia testing, the Black Panther Party created many more programs. They created a free ambulance program, free dental program, free health clinics, nutrition classes, police patrols to monitor police brutality, clothing distribution, classes on politics and economics, classes on self-defense and first aid, transportation to upstate prisons for family members of inmates, and drug and alcohol rehabilitation.

On behalf of all the Black Panthers- You're welcome!

Notable Figures of the **Black Panther** Party · Huey P. Newton · Bobby Seale · Angela Davis · Eldridge Cleaver · Elaine Brown · Stokely Carmichael · Fred Hampton.

Thank you for your sacrifices and your service.

PANTHER
POWER TO THE PEOPLE...
THEN AND NOW

Original six members of the Black Panther Party (1966)

Top left to right: Elbert "Big Man" Howard, Huey P. Newton (Defense Minister), Sherwin Forte, Bobby Seale (Chairman)
Bottom: Reggie Forte and Little Bobby Hutton (Treasurer).

Bobby Seale A Black Panther Co-Founder:

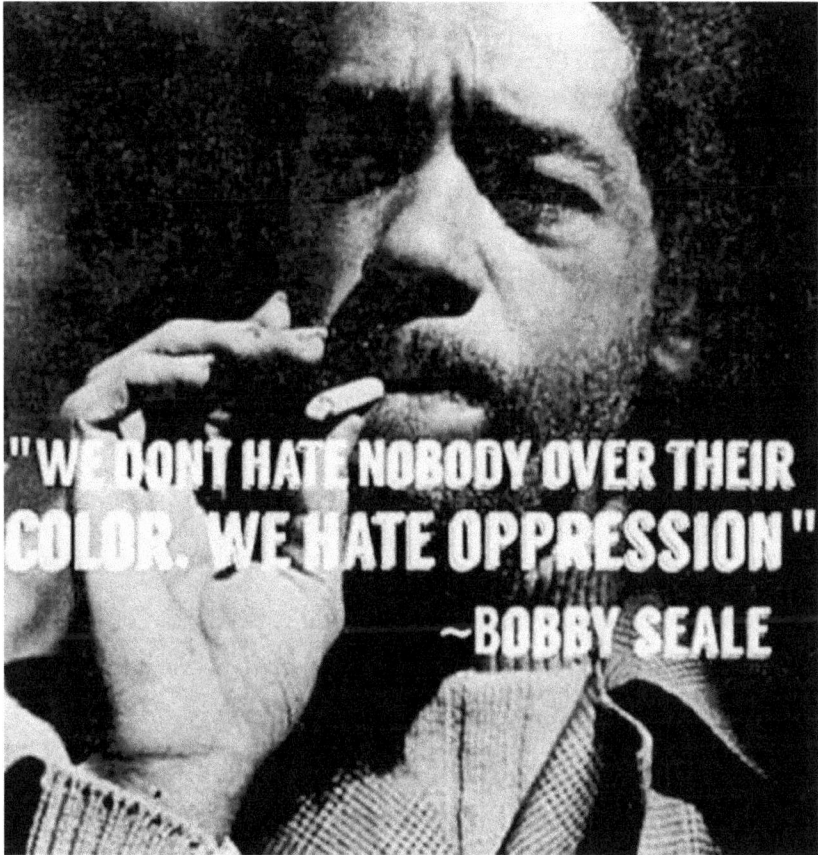

"WE DONT HATE NOBODY OVER THEIR COLOR. WE HATE OPPRESSION" ~BOBBY SEALE

Chapter

3

Limitless Talent
Entertaining the World

❧

"Swag on 10"

I truly love that free expression is not only allowed and accepted in America but encouraged, and boy, did my people run with that!

From the time we were "set free" until the present day, no one has serenaded and amazed the world with our natural musical prowess and our effortless domination of the entertainment world.

Wherever I venture into the world or almost everywhere in the United States, no matter the establishment, you will hear some sort of Foundational Black American music playing in the background.

I was recently in Cabo airport at STK, and it was so nice to hear oldies playing in the background; they were playing old school Rhythm and blues.

A few months before that, I was in an all-white area in Los Angeles in a high-end bar with 95 percent of the crowd being white, and you guessed it -they were playing American black music.

From commercials to weddings to background music in the grocery store, more often than not, my people will be tantalizing your eardrums- your welcome.

This is an amazing feat in itself when in less than 100 years, we went from being in chains treated like livestock to total world domination in the entertainment industry.

We are the most recognized names and talent worldwide, whether in music, comedy, or sports, our swag has no competition. The only music that comes close to serenading the world in the way we do would be reggae – but I will have a section on that later.

Slavery officially "ended" in 1865, and less than 50 years later, you had an explosion of talent!

We are the epitome of Black Excellence.

Or as we like to say...

"Aint nothing to it, but to do it."

The Harlem Renaissance was an intellectual and cultural revival of Foundational Black American music, dance, art, fashion, literature, theater, and politics centered in Harlem, Manhattan, New York City, spanning the 1920s and 1930s.

In 1915 and 1916, natural disasters in the south put Black workers and sharecroppers out of work. Additionally, during and after World War I, immigration to the United States fell, and northern recruiters headed south to entice Black workers to their companies.

By 1920, some 300,000 Foundational Black Americans from the South had moved north, and Harlem was one of the most popular destinations for these families.

Great Migration

The northern Manhattan neighborhood of Harlem was meant to be an upper-class white neighborhood in the 1880s, but rapid overdevelopment led to empty buildings and desperate property owners seeking to fill them.

In the early 1900s, a few middle-class Black families from another neighborhood known as Black Bohemia moved to Harlem, and other Black families followed. Some white residents initially fought to keep Black Americans out of the area but failing that, many whites eventually fled.

Growing up in an all-black environment, one thing we would say all the time is "all we got is space and opportunity." Considering how fast my people went from ashy to classy, this is true, as soon as we had the space and opportunity, we took over!

Many great musicians came out of New York as suspected because it has a very diverse and unique culture and makeup compared to most other places.

New York is a literal Gumbo of people and especially people of color, so, of course, you will get some of the most flavorful products.

You can credit and thank the Harlem Renaissance for some of the most prolific founders of black talent, writing, and music today.

People such as:

Louis Armstrong- American trumpeter and vocalist one of the most influential figures in jazz

Dorothy Dandridge – First black woman to be nominated for an academy award

Dizzy Gillespie- American jazz trumpeter, bandleader, composer, educator, and singer

Duke Ellington – American composer, pianist, and leader of a jazz orchestra

Bessie Smith – Empress of the Blues

Billy Holiday – American Jazz and swing music Singer

Ma Rainy – Mother of blues

Ella Fitzgerald – Queen of Jazz

Buddy Bolden – Father of Jazz

This is a very short list, but we all owe these pioneers a thank you for persevering through the worst of times to create something timeless for us all to enjoy.

We often use a foundational black American colloquialism, which is "flip the script." I can't think of a more amazing example of this than foundational black America that in less than 50 years changed the landscape of American music with zero help from anyone.

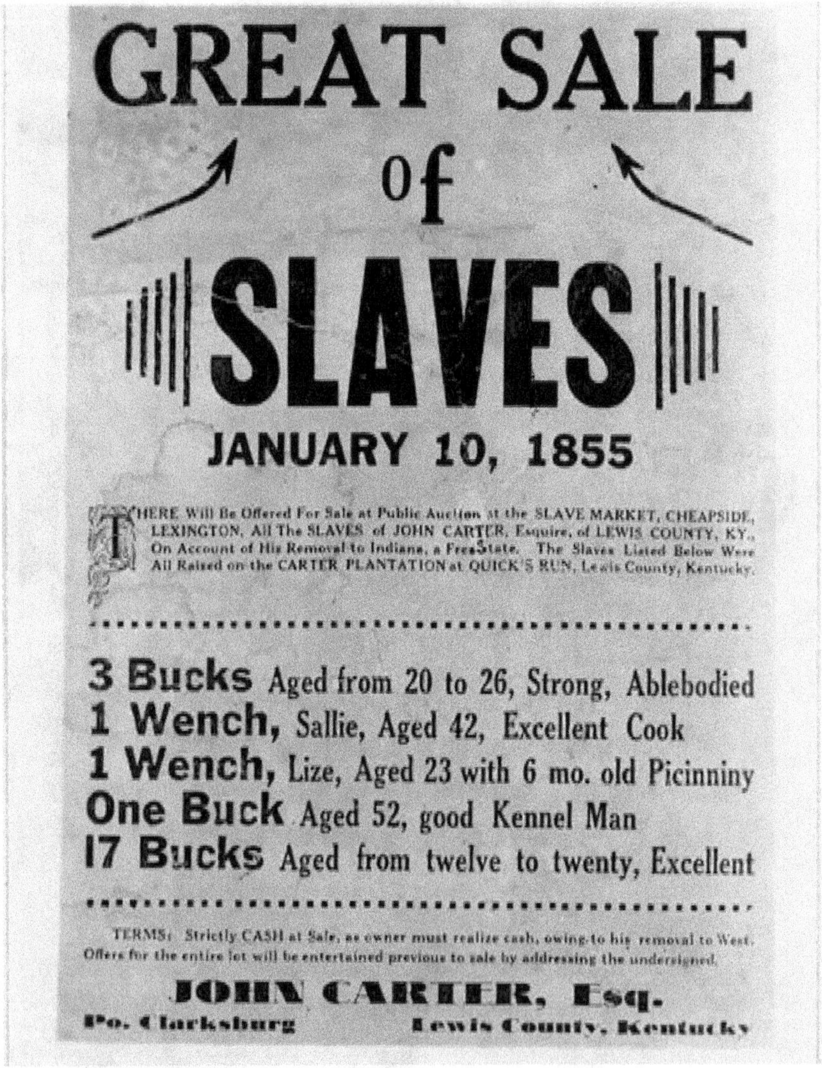
GREAT SALE
of
SLAVES
JANUARY 10, 1855
THERE Will Be Offered For Sale at Public Auction at the SLAVE MARKET, CHEAPSIDE, LEXINGTON, All The SLAVES of JOHN CARTER, Esquire, of LEWIS COUNTY, KY., On Account of His Removal to Indiana, a Free State. The Slaves Listed Below Were All Raised on the CARTER PLANTATION at QUICK'S RUN, Lewis County, Kentucky.
3 Bucks Aged from 20 to 26, Strong, Ablebodied
1 Wench, Sallie, Aged 42, Excellent Cook
1 Wench, Lize, Aged 23 with 6 mo. old Picinniny
One Buck Aged 52, good Kennel Man
17 Bucks Aged from twelve to twenty, Excellent
TERMS: Strictly CASH at Sale, as owner must realize cash, owing to his removal to West. Offers for the entire lot will be entertained previous to sale by addressing the undersigned.
JOHN CARTER, Esq.
Po. Clarksburg
Lewis County, Kentucky

There have been no other people in history with a comeback like ours.

We did it with style, grace, and talent.

Hip Hop and Rap is as American as it gets.

Sylvia Robinson is known as Hip-Hop's First Godmother. She was the founder of Sugar Hill Records and helped produce the first popular mainstream rap song, "Rappers Delight," by the Sugar Hill Gang. Sylvia Robinson created the template for hip-hop's world domination, from the first rap single to sell a million to the first scratching on record. Her genius for production built an empire.

This Genre of music is now a global phenomenon (stating the obvious), but before it was that it was the gumbo in New York that started the base for the roux for this flavor of music EVERYONE loves.

I would be remiss not to point out, this is one of the reasons this type of music is so great is because its many influences from Caribbean culture and other black people (even though non-American) their unique influences of rhythm and musical talents mixed with ours has proven to be an unstoppable force.

But before Sylvia and anyone else even thought of talking over beats, we had a musical genius that was rapping or speaking over beats way back in the day named Dewey "Pigmeat" Markham was an American entertainer. Though best known as a comedian, Markham was also a singer, dancer, and actor. His nickname came from a stage routine, in which he declared himself to be "Sweet Poppa Pigmeat." He was sometimes credited in films as Pigmeat "Alamo," born in 1917 in North Carolina. He was rapping before we even knew what rap and hip hop were.

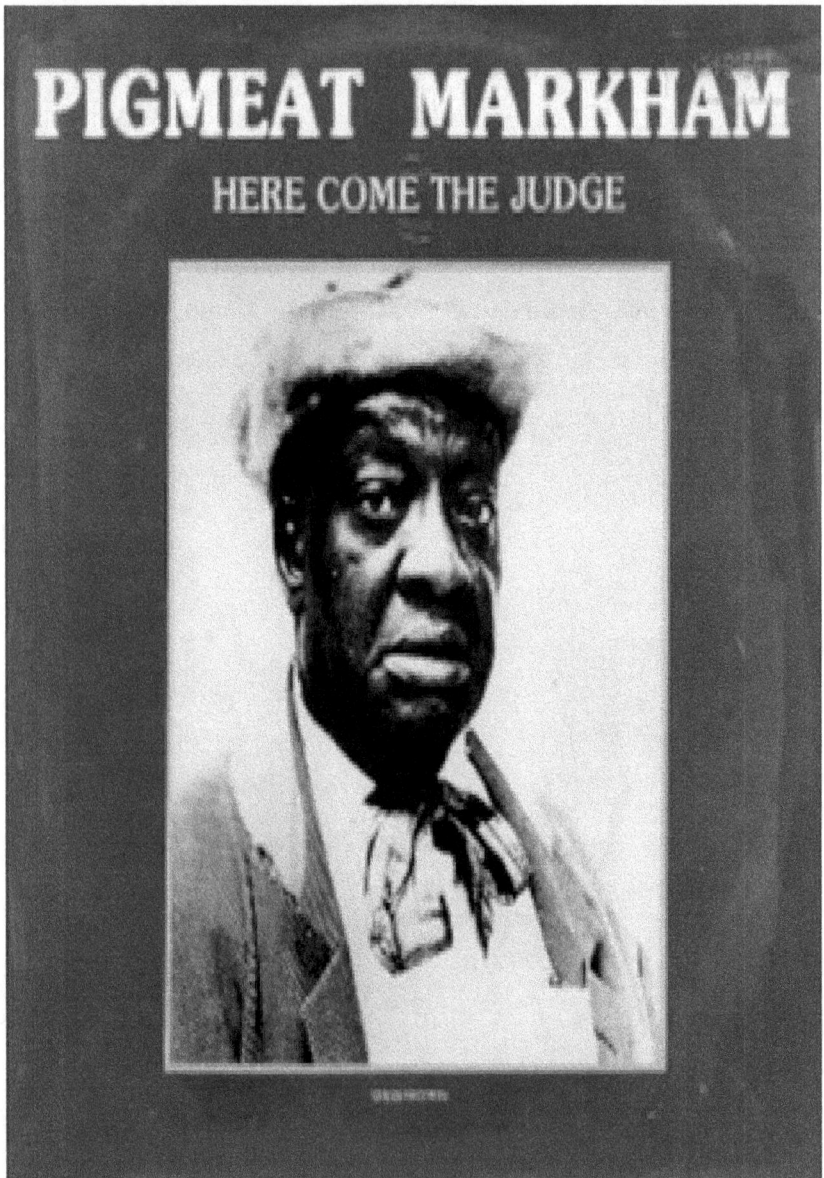

Some of the most timeless, soulful, soothing, and happy music you will hear comes from the mid-west in the 1960s and 1970s — which we affectionally call Soul music today known as Neo-soul. The predominantly Foundational Black American Artists listed below are literal American treasures that can change your whole mood with one song.

Marvin Gaye

Aretha Franklin

James Brown

Stevie Wonder

Otis Redding

Al Green

Ray Charles

Sam Cooke

The temptations

Smokey Robinson

Curtis Mayfield

The Supremes

Wilson Pickett

Isaac Hayes

Etta James

The Isley Brothers

Diana Ross

Percy Sledge

Earth, Wind & Fire

The Ojays

The Jackson 5

Chaka Khan

Four tops

Bobby Womack

The Staple Singers

Patti Labelle

Sly and the Family Stine

Whitney Houston

Luther Vandross

Mary J Blige

Erykah Badu

Jill Scott

Prince

Michael Jackson

HAZEL SCOTT, PIANO PRODIGY, AGE 4 [1920S]. SHE HAD NO LESSONS, BUT COULD REPLICATE EVERYTHING SHE HEARD. ACCEPTED INTO JUILLIARD AT 8, SHE WAS AN INT'L JAZZ STAR BY 25 (REFUSING TO PLAY FOR SEGREGATED AUDIENCES), THEN THE FIRST BLACK PERSON TO HOST THEIR OWN TV SHOW.

BLACK CULTURE NEWS.

As you can see, most of these people are superstars known for serenading the world with their beautiful soul healing voices, music, and talent- Your welcome.

When the powers that be realized the healing power of music through frequencies, they introduced a new form of "black music" that mostly dominates the airwaves today, and it has the exact opposite effect of healing the soul.

Listen to any of the artists I named and pay attention to how you feel in your soul while listening to them and how you feel afterward.

Now pick any song on the top ten list today and do the same – if you are still connected to the source energy of your soul, you will feel a stark difference. It will start to become clear why our youth and the world is in the state is in today.

DID YOU KNOW?

JIMI HENDRIX, along with JOHN LENNON, Bob Marley and Prince all tuned their music to a specific FREQUENCY OF 432Hz!
It is known as the "BEAT OF THE EARTH", has substantial HEALING benefits and ancient Egyptian and Greek instruments were discovered tuned to 432Hz. However, since 1953 all music has been tuned to 440Hz. This frequency has NO SCIENTIFIC RELATIONSHIP with our universe and actually causes the brain to become agitated. The Nazis in WW2 used this frequency against their enemies to make them feel and think a certain way. @HolisticMedicine4u

Nevertheless, whatever we do, we dominate and influence. You know, I saw a show where they are beatboxing in Morocco?? Well, as they say, imitation is the sincerest form of flattery.

I love seeing our influence being imitated worldwide! Do your thing!!

But at the same time, the respect for the people who invented it must be there, as good relationships are reciprocal with respect.

With respect, we can all eat together; without it, you're just another biter wannabe.

Influences in Telllievision.

blacks.united

We need this again.

668 likes

blacks.united Yesss - Buy1Get1Free Tap Link In Bio @blacks.united 🤍 Follow @blacks.united for... more

View all 8 comments

Fun fact: Did you know when the show "A Different World" was on television that HBCU enrollment shot up almost 40 percent?

This, if nothing else, should explain the power of television- it is called programming for a reason.

There is also a reason we don't see wholesome black family shows anymore like we did before as television sets the tone for society on what is normal and acceptable behavior.

The African American culture is being secretly negatively steered through negative media social engineering.

A group's identity is shaped by how they see themselves repeatedly depicted within the media. People often becomes those derogatory media depictions of their group that they accept as being their reality. Therefore those who controls a people's media images controls their culture. It's a true hidden science known as media social engineering. Because the white society controls the media images of African Americans, this allows white social scientists to negatively steer our culture. It's the true reason why millions of African Americans now self identifies as N!ggers, regards Black women as Bitches and Hoes, sag their pants, and glorifies pimps. - Franklin Jones

www.theblackpeoplesmatrix.com

**PROOF
THAT THE BRAINWASHING
AND CONDITIONING IS
WORKING ON OUR PEOPLE**

I remember being a small child, maybe 5 or 6 years old, in my grandmother's living room, sitting on the floor playing while my grandmother, my uncle josh (My grandmothers' brother), And my daddy were all sitting around watching TV and talking. A commercial that was selling knives came on, and of course, you know how it goes; the Tv was saying these are the best knives in history!

My Uncle Josh said, "Shiiii them dang knives are probably rusty by the time they even make it to your house!"

Then, everyone, of course, laughed.

Then my daddy turned to me and said, "Carolyn Jo, don't you EVER, and I mean, EVER believe ANYTHING you hear on the Tell lie vision without doing your own research first! I don't even care if it's on the news. DO NOT EVER TAKE IT FOR FACE VALUE because all they do is LIE!"

I was a small child, so all I said was "yes, Daddy," but that message stuck with me.

"..the press is manipulating everything that's been happening... They do not tell the truth. They are lying. They manipulate our history books. The history books are not true. It's a lie. The history books are lying, you need to know that, you must know that"

- #Michael Jackson

"I ain't draft dodging. I ain't burning no flag. I ain't running to Canada. I'm staying right here. You want to send me to jail? Fine, you go right ahead. I've been in jail for 400 years. I could be there for four or five more, but I ain't going no 10,000 miles to help murder and kill other poor people.

"If I want to die, I'll die right here, right now, fightin' you, if I want to die. You my enemy, not no Chinese, no Vietcong, no Japanese. You my opposer when I want freedom. You my opposer when I want justice. You my opposer when I want equality. Want me to go somewhere and fight for you? You won't even stand up for me right here in America, for my rights and my religious beliefs. You won't even stand up for me right here at home. "

- Muhammad Ali

The problem with the entertainment industry today is the same thing that happens with the civil rights movement.

It has been infiltrated with evil and no longer serves the interest of the people.

We call them celebrities and politicians.

Some slaughterhouses use a "Judas goat." It's a trained goat that will calmly lead livestock to their slaughter while its own life is spared.

Now, I am not going to sit here and act holier than thou, like I don't listen to new school music or watch new age shows. I do.

And I absolutely love "turning up" when the time calls for it or enjoying a new movie or a new television show.

But at the same time, I am very aware of the programming, and take everything with a grain of salt.

I also try my best to never imitate or look to "stars" as leaders- THEY ARE NOT.

They are nothing more than entertainers, let them entertain you, but never let them advise you or rule over you.

Unless you want to be led astray.

"When we see a black man who is constantly being praised by the Americans, begin to suspect him. When we see a black man get honors and all sorts of decorations and the United States flatters him with fine words and phrases, immediately suspect that person. Because our experience has taught us that the Americans do not exalt any black man that is really working for the benefit of the black man." (Malcolm X)

Foundational Black Americans

have contributed so much to America and

to the world.

How have we been Thanked?

Part

2

Make Amends

The next three chapters will go over just some of the ways we have been thanked or repaid thus far for all our wonderful contributions to this world.

Chapter

4

Dehumanized

—❖—

"Their depravity knows no depths."

People will have all kinds of feelings about the next few chapters and the things I will go over; let me assure you of two things...

1. What I am covering is just the tip of the iceberg.

2. I know the truth can feel uncomfortable – but imagine how uncomfortable it was to *LIVE through it.*

Lest never forget

This chapter will go over how we didn't have body autonomy and how our bodies have been used and abused right here in the USA for centuries.

Can you name one other group of people that went through this for centuries while the United States was being built?

My heritage is unique, and no one has paid a higher price in the United States than Foundational Black Americans; this is my Land and my Country.

Millie Williams

"Talkin' 'bout somethin' awful, you should have been dere. De slave owners was shoutin' and sellin' chillen to one man and de mamma and pappy to 'nother. De slaves cries and takes on somethin' awful. If a woman had lots of chillen she was sold for mo', cause it a sign she a good breeder."

Story/ Blogpost about Millie Williams stealing a chicken.

When I hold my baby in my arms I do it like it is a sacred privilege knowing that so many of my Ancestors' babies were snatched away from their arms never to be seen again.

Breeding Farms

—––—
❖

I am one internship away from having a master's degree- meaning I have my bachelor's and I have completed all my coursework for my Masters; however, I was never taught how, right here in the United States, Foundational Black Americans were made to breed with each other just like livestock.

I can see why the United States would want to erase this from its history but then just be aware of yourself, that some formally educated people are truly uninformed and naive by design.

Formal education has become nothing more than indoctrination centers. The truly educated and informed have done independent research and studies and have educated themselves.

The slave population of the breeding farm was mostly women and children not matured enough to be sold, and a limited number of men whose job was to impregnate as many slave women as possible. All the breeders wanted was a child that could be sold.

Nobody talks about the 13-year-old girl on a breeding farm, forced to bear as many children as possible, only to have them ripped away and sent down South to endure a lifetime of hardship without a mother. On some breeding farm, the mother would be freed after birthing fifteen children. What would she have to look forward to?

When enslaved males turned 15 years old–and younger in some cases–they had their first inspection. Boys who were under-developed had their testicles castrated and sent to the market or used on the farm. Each enslaved male was expected to get 12 females pregnant a year. The men were used for breeding for five years. One enslaved man named Burt produced more than 200 offspring, according to the *Slave Narratives*.

America barely acknowledges that breeding farms existed, let alone document their role in creating the robust economy of the early South. There are the self-evident truths mentioned in the Declaration of Independence, and those truths so heinous they must perpetually be covered up and denied.

Those slaves who outlived the period were permanently scarred for life.

Through the harrowing tales of captivity, maltreatment, and dehumanization, the enslaved men certainly lost their sense of identity and masculinity.

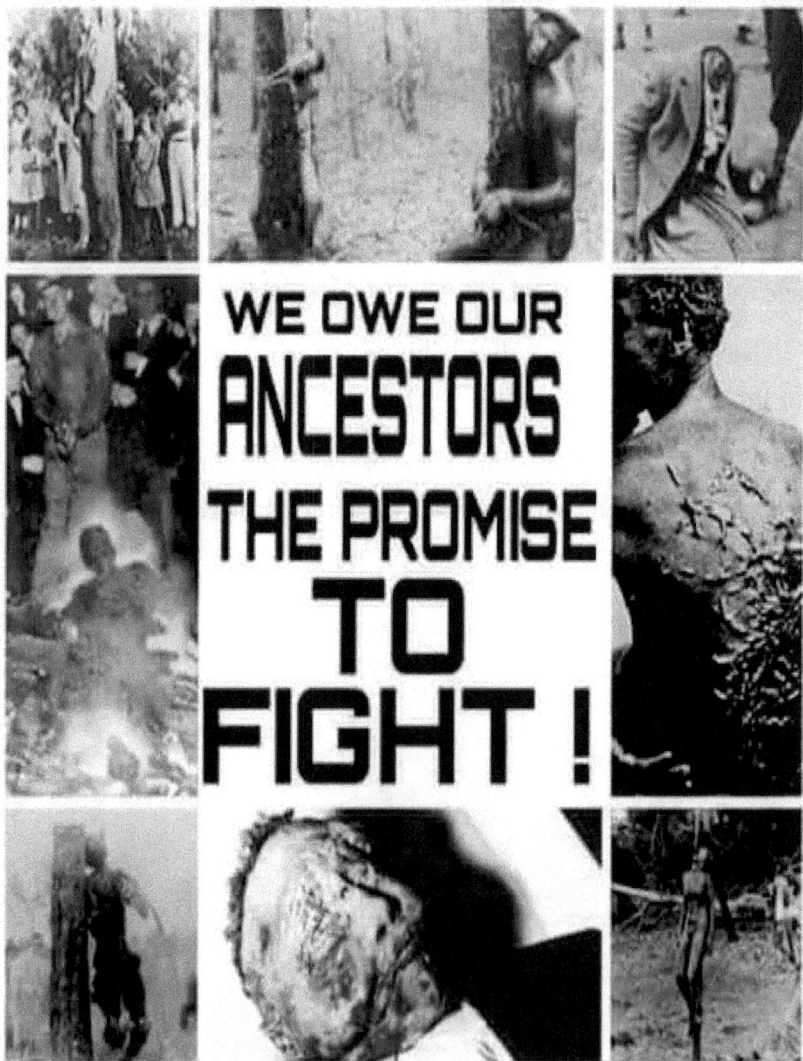

Oshun Bunmi Ogundipe
⬡ Admin • 33 mins • 👥

I never will... It's still happening but with guns now... 😔 👿

Our DNA is literally traumatized at the hands of the
American government and the Elite.

MAKE AMENDS!

Buck Breaking

Origin Of Buck Breaking

Buck Breaking came to life when African slaves' rebellions had increased. It first started with the stripping of male slaves and flogging them while other slaves watched. With time, it graduated into stripping and raping them. This act spared no males; it affected both children and men.

At a time, Buck Breaking became so successful that it grew into "sex farms" where male African slaves were bred just for the purpose of being raped by their white masters.

Buck Breaking was done to cripple the ego and strength of the male slaves. Most slaves, after being raped, committed suicide as they could not "live with the shame."

Buck Breaking was also done in the presence of little male slaves and the male slaves' families to show the superiority of the white master over the male slave. Buck Breaking crippled most little revolutions, making slaves weak and less motivated. It broke the spirit of African male slaves and made them feel less masculine.

The Buck Breaking story wasn't discussed during those days as male slaves felt their egos bruised, so they avoided talking about their encounters and experiences. Buck Breaking is just one of the many ways prisoners of war were punished and controlled. Buck breaking was also mixed with the "breeding farms" business white supremacists and slave owners operated. Breeding farms were created to increase the population of black people forcefully.

This practice was a very physically heinous act, but the true intention was to break the people mentally, especially the children so they would never even think of escaping. Everything starts in the mind. If you break a person's mind, you break their spirit, and most will easily just resolve that this is their fate.

THIS IS OUR TRUTH AT THE HANDS OF WHITE
AMERICA. LIKE 911, LET US NEVER FORGET

I love America- but she owes Foundational Native Black Americans everything for her very existence.

Made into purses

✜

The Nat Turner rebellion

In 1831 a slave named Nat Turner led a rebellion in Southampton County, Virginia. A religious leader and self-styled Baptist minister, Turner, and a group of followers killed sixty white men, women, and children on the night of August 21. Turner and 16 of his conspirators were captured and executed, but the incident continued to haunt Southern whites. Native Black people were randomly killed all over Southampton County; many were beheaded, and their heads left along the roads to warn others. In the wake of the uprising, planters tightened their grip on slaves and slavery.

To instill even more mental control and torture over foundational black American prisoners of war even after we were dead, our bodies were turned into objects, and parts of us kept as momentous as a reminder of what would happen to you if you would even think of attempting to try and change the status quo.

Turner's body did not receive a formal burial, but details about what happened to the body are unknown. According to several reports, as Tony Horwitz reported in the *New Yorker*, the rebel leader's corpse was given to doctors for dissection, and his body parts were distributed among white families. As recounted by John W. Cromwell in a 1920 article in the *Journal of Negro History*, "Turner was skinned to supply such souvenirs as purses, his flesh made into grease, and his bones divided as trophies to be handed down as heirlooms."

⟲ Author Leah Yehudah Retweeted

Shaft
@WisecraQUE3

Nat Turner was skinned, cooked, and eaten by white people. white people also boiled his body down into a liquid and drank his remains in an elixir called "Nat's Grease" (Curry, 2017; New York Times, 1860)

the Devil can't make this up.

twitter.com/mysticxlipstic...

> **Ayoka** ✓ @MysticxLipstick · 1d
> Yes we visited the county and got a tour where the Nat Turner Revolt happened and they even turned us into lampshades. This is where picnics came from. Pick a n*gger where they tortured us, hung us, ate us and skinned us.
> Show this thread

Black baby alligator bait

Alligator bait, also known as gator bait, was the practice of using black infant children as bait to lure alligators. It was done by white men during slavery in Florida, Louisiana, and other parts of the American South.

In 1923 'Time magazine' carried this story: From Chipley, Fla., it was reported that colored babies were being used for alligator bait. The infants were left to play in shallow water while expert shooters watched from nearby concealment. It was widely reported in the American press, so it was at least believable among white Americans of the time.

Film: The practice has appeared in at least two films: "Alligator Bait" (1900) and "The 'Gator and the Pickaninny" (1900). Two tales of boys used as alligator bait were told in "Untamed Fury" (1947).

Probably from at least the 1860's up until the 1960's "alligator bait" was a racial slur among whites for little black children. In Harlem, in the 1940's it was applied to blacks of any age from Florida.

It is hard to process the thinking that could lead a person to use a live human baby as bait for an alligator. That is why the objects in the Jim Crow Museum are so important – they help tell the story of a society that defined African Americans as "sub-human" by portraying them as savage and worthless creatures ("Americans Forced" 1944). If people are indoctrinated, repeatedly, with items, images, objects, and practices that devalue the humanity of African Americans, then practices like African Dodgers, Human Zoos, and Alligator bait become possible.

ALLIGATOR BAIT

ALLIGATOR HUNTING WAS VERY PROFITABLE IN THE 1800-1900'S. THE SKINS WERE USED TO MAKE SHOES, BAGS, BELTS AND OTHER ITEMS. HOWEVER, WHITE HUNTERS OFTEN LOST THEIR ARMS AND SOMETIMES THEIR LIVES AS THEY RUSTLED THE SWAMPY WATERS AT NIGHT ATTEMPTING TO ATTRACT ALLIGATORS TO THE SURFACE, SO THEY DECIDED TO USE SLAVE BABIES AS BAIT. THIS HORRENDOUS ACT WAS LATER CHARACTERIZED IN SHEET MUSIC, POST CARDS AND FIGURINES. YEARS LATER, A CANDY MANUFACTURER OF BLACK LICORICE DROPS CREATED A DISTASTEFUL ADVERTISEMENT THAT FEATURED A HUNGRY LOOKING ALLIGATOR LEERING AT A BUG-EYED BLACK BABY. THE AD READ: *A DAINTY LITTLE MORSEL"* *FOR DECADES*, THE POPULAR CANDY WAS REFERRED TO AS *"NIGGER BABIES"*. THE NAME WAS LATER CHANGED TO "NIBS" AND IS STILL ON THE MARKET TODAY.

LEST WE FORGET BLACK HOLOCAUST MUSEUM

P J. Marion Sims – purchased black women slaves as Guinea pigs

❧

"J. Marion Sims was a gynecologist in the 1800s who purchased native Black women slaves/ prisoners of war and used them as guinea pigs for his untested surgical experiments. He repeatedly performed genital surgery on Black women WITHOUT ANESTHESIA because, according to him, 'Black women don't feel pain.' Despite his inhumane tests on Black women, Sims was named 'the father of modern gynecology,' and his statue currently stands right outside of the New York Academy of Medicine.

Of course, they appeared to feel no pain; the feelings were beat out of them and their mother and father daily for centuries.

Also, when we say take down statues of hate, this is a perfect example of what we mean.

Make Amends.

Literal Lab rats

❧

Growing up in Los Angeles, everyone knew what hospitals to go to and which not to go to. In Los Angeles, everyone knew not to go to "Killer King."

As I have moved here and there over the years, I have come to understand black people everywhere in the United States have a certain hospital with a reputation of people going there with minor ailments and mysteriously never checking out.

"That day in Erika Johnson's high-school biology class, some 20 years ago, is seared into her memory. The teacher was leading the students through experiments involving cells from a widely used line known as HeLa. The cell line originated from tissue taken from a woman named Henrietta Lacks — and Johnson's mother was a Lacks. "This is my great-grandmother I'm holding in my hand," Johnson remembers feeling. "It was a very surreal situation."

Last month marked 100 years since Lacks's birth. She died in 1951, aged 31, of an aggressive cervical cancer. Months earlier, doctors at the Johns Hopkins Hospital in Baltimore, Maryland, had taken samples of her cancerous cells while diagnosing and treating the disease. They gave some of that tissue to a researcher without Lacks's knowledge or consent. In the laboratory, her cells turned out to have an extraordinary ability to survive and reproduce; they were, in essence, immortal. The researcher shared them widely with other scientists, becoming a workhorse of biological research. Today, work done with HeLa cells underpins much of modern medicine; they have been involved in key discoveries in many fields, including cancer, immunology, and infectious disease.

But the story of Henrietta Lacks also illustrates the racial inequities embedded in the US research and healthcare systems. Lacks was a Native Black woman. The hospital where her cells were collected was one of only a few that supplied medical care to Black people. None of the biotechnology or other companies that profited from her cells passed any money back to her family. And, for decades after her death, doctors and scientists repeatedly did not ask her family for consent as they revealed Lacks's name publicly, gave her medical records to the media, and even published her cells' genome online. (Following an outcry, the genome was soon removed.) *Nature* later published the genome of another HeLa line1 after the Lacks family reached an agreement with the US National Institutes of Health (NIH) to approve its release.

The history of human experimentation is as old as the practice of medicine and in the modern era has always targeted disadvantaged, marginalized, institutionalized, stigmatized, and vulnerable populations: prisoners, the condemned, orphans, the mentally ill, students, the poor, women, the disabled, children, peoples of color, indigenous peoples and the enslaved.

Human subject research is clear wherever physicians, technicians, pharmaceutical companies (and others) are trialing new practices and implementing the latest diagnostic and therapeutic agents and procedures. And the American South in the days of slavery was no different – and for those looking for easy targets, black slave bodies were easy to come by.

Black Bodies in The Slave South

There is a rich and rapidly expanding scholarly literature examining the history of human subject research, including studies of the burgeoning bio-medical economy in the US in the 20th century. The Tuskegee experiment and other episodes of medical racism all feature prominently.

The history of the acquisition and exploitation of slave bodies for medical education and research in the US, first explored in depth by historians James Breeden and Todd Savitt, focused primarily on medical schools and the traffic in slave bodies in Virginia. Savitt's work drew attention to professional medicine's use of slaves in classrooms, bedside demonstrations, operating amphitheaters, and experimental facilities.

Savitt argued that African Americans were easy targets for ambitious and entrepreneurial white physicians in the slave south. Slaves, as human commodities, were readily transformed into a medical resource, easily accessible as empirical test subjects, "voiceless," and rendered "medically incompetent" through the joint power and authority of the enslaver and their employee, the white physician. Savitt suggested that "outright experimentation upon living humans may have occurred more openly and perhaps more often owing to the nature of slave society," and also that "the situation may have been (and probably was) worse in the Deep South."

Power And Opportunism

When an elite white enslaver-physician, Charlestonian Elias S. Bennett, published notes recalling the case of a truly extraordinary tumor afflicting a young female slave on the family's James Island plantation, his narrative revealed a lot about the opportunities for human subject research under American slavery.

Bennett recalled an unnamed female patient who had developed "a small tumor the size of a ten-cent piece" behind her right ear when she was four weeks old. In 1817, when Bennett was training to become a doctor and "anxious to perform an operation," he, together with a fellow physician-apprentice, made a disastrously crude surgical attempt to explore and remove this growth.

In an era prior to anesthesia and asepsis, this type of surgical intervention was extremely dangerous – especially when undertaken by two unsupervised medical apprentices – who took the liberty of an opportunity presented by an extremely vulnerable enslaved child. As Bennett remembered, the child suffered a great deal of "inflammation" as a result, and only "by very close attention" did she recover "in six to eight weeks" – the plantation/labor camp's seclusion providing perfect cover for what would prove to be a major medical blunder.

Unknown enslaved sufferer'. Waring Historical Library, Charleston

Bennett's crude interference with the tumor, which may have been in a lymph node, was the cause of a severe inflammatory reaction and sudden excessive growth of the lesion. In 1821, when the child was six, Bennett described the tumor as being about the size of an ostrich egg. In the years prior to her death, his narrative reported that the tumor increased to an enormous, indeed "extraordinary" size. The case report concludes with a post-mortem analysis, or, as Bennett noted in a ghoulish tone, "an imperfect outline of the results furnished by the examination of the tumor, when I obtained the head or at least so much of it as remained."

The remains of the enslaved girl's skull became a pathological specimen in the University of Maryland's medical museum collection.

Dark Medicine: Cash For 'Negros'

All the key training, networks, and power bases of southern medicine—apprenticeships, private practice, colleges, hospitals, journals, and societies—operated through slavery's ruthless traffic and exploitation of black bodies. White medical students expected education and training based on the observation, dissection, and experimental treatment of black bodies.

White doctors, including those in remote rural locations, routinely sent reports of experiments on slave subjects to medical journals and trafficked black bodies to medical colleges. Medical museums openly asked for black body parts and medical societies relied on black bodies. Students too wrote graduating theses based on the medical manipulation of black "subjects" and "specimens."

Under slavery, there was also an extensive network of specialist "negro hospitals." The grimmest of slavery's institutions, these hospitals, were often sites of risky medical research and were closely linked to "negro traders" anxious to patch up their "stock" for sale. Large numbers of individual doctors routinely advertised in southern newspapers that they would pay cash for black people suffering from chronic disease. The fate of these trafficked medical subjects, of course, assumed the very worst possibilities.

Slaves were generally unable to prevent treatments chosen by their owners, and physicians could take enormous risks with the lives of these patients. Those risks were all the greater when doctors were also the owners of the enslaved patients. The opportunities presented by the system of chattel slavery meant that white doctors had at hand an easily accessible population upon which they could execute experimental research programs and develop new tools, techniques, and medicines.

White racist attitudes, the enormous traffic in human chattel, and the slave regime rationalized and normalized the use and abuse of black bodies. Human subject research under American slavery was ultimately nothing unusual. In the context of a society defined by dehumanization, impoverishment, violent punishment, incarceration, a vigorous trade in human property, racialization, and sexual interference, it should come as no surprise that human experimentation and the exploitation of enslaved bodies was a frequent, widespread, and indeed commonplace feature of medical encounters between physicians and slaves. That was the culture of American slavery, and every day, slave patients faced appalling dangers.

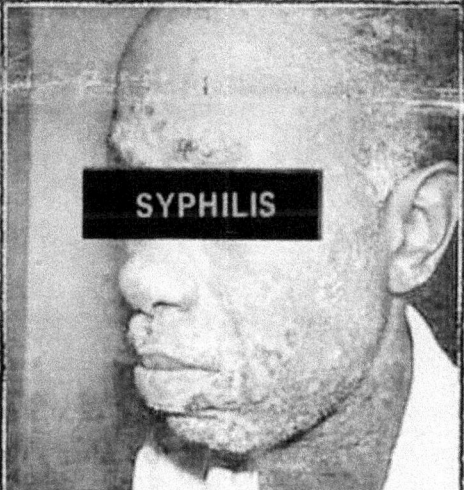

THE BLACK PANTHER

INTERCOMMUNAL NEWS SERVICE 25cents

THE BLACK PANTHER PARTY

GERM WARFARE DECLARED AGAINST BLACKS!

HUNDREDS OF BLACK MEN DISCOVERED MASSACRED IN SYPHILIS "EXPERIMENT".

SEE ARTICLE INSIDE PAGE 2

SYPHILIS

Agent Orange

❧

Agent Orange was a powerful herbicide used by U.S. military forces during the Vietnam War to eliminate forest cover and crops for North Vietnamese and Viet Cong troops. The U.S. program, codenamed Operation Ranch Hand, sprayed more than 20 million gallons of various herbicides over Vietnam, Cambodia, and Laos from 1961 to 1971. Agent Orange, which contained the deadly chemical dioxin, was the most used herbicide. It was later proven to cause serious health issues—including cancer, birth defects, rashes, and severe psychological and neurological problems—among the Vietnamese people as well as among returning U.S. servicemen and their families.

From 1961 to 1971, the U.S. military sprayed a range of herbicides across more than 4.5 million acres of Vietnam to destroy the forest cover and food crops used by enemy North Vietnamese and Viet Cong troops.

U.S. aircraft were deployed to douse roads, rivers, canals, rice paddies, and farmland with powerful mixtures of herbicides. During this process, crops and water sources used by the non-combatant native population of South Vietnam were also hit.

In all, American forces used more than 20 million gallons of herbicides in Vietnam, Laos, and Cambodia during the years of Operation Ranch Hand. Herbicides were also sprayed from trucks and hand-sprayers around U.S. military bases.

Some military personnel during the Vietnam War era joked that "Only you can prevent a forest," a twist on the U.S. Forest Service's popular fire-fighting campaign featuring Smokey the Bear.

Effects of Agent Orange

Because Agent Orange (and other Vietnam-era herbicides) contained dioxin in the form of TCDD, it had immediate and long-term effects.

Dioxin is a highly persistent chemical compound that lasts for many years in the environment, particularly in soil, lake, river sediments, and the food chain. Dioxin accumulates in fatty tissue in the bodies of fish, birds, and other animals. Most human exposure is through foods such as meats, poultry, dairy products, eggs, shellfish, and fish.

Studies on laboratory animals have proven that dioxin is highly toxic, even in minute doses. It is universally known to be a carcinogen (a cancer-causing agent).

Short-term exposure to dioxin can cause darkening of the skin, liver problems, and a severe acne-like skin disease called chloracne. Additionally, dioxin is linked to type 2 diabetes, immune system dysfunction, nerve disorders, muscular dysfunction, hormone disruption, and heart disease.

Developing fetuses are particularly sensitive to dioxin, which is also linked to miscarriages, spina bifida, and other fetal brain and nervous system development problems.

Veteran Health Issues and Legal Battle

Questions about Agent Orange arose in the United States after an increasing number of returning Vietnam veterans and their families began to report a range of afflictions, including rashes and other skin irritations, miscarriages, psychological symptoms, type 2 diabetes, birth defects in children, and cancers such as Hodgkin's disease, prostate cancer, and leukemia.

In 1988, Dr. James Clary, an Air Force researcher associated with Operation Ranch Hand, wrote to Senator Tom Daschle, "When we started the herbicide program in the 1960s, we were aware of the potential for damage due to dioxin contamination in the herbicide. However, because the material was to be used on the enemy, none of us were overly concerned. We never considered a scenario in which our own personnel would become contaminated with the herbicide."

In 1979, a class-action lawsuit was filed on behalf of 2.4 million veterans exposed to Agent Orange during their service in Vietnam. Five years later, in an out-of-court settlement, seven large chemical companies that manufactured the herbicide agreed to pay $180 million in compensation to the veterans or their next of kin.

My father, a foundational black American, was affected by Agent Orange while he served his country in Vietnam.

Chemical warfare is nothing new, my condolences to the Vietnamese.

When they say all is fair in love and war, they mean it literally. Trust me when I tell you just as great the United States is also how corrupt it is.

The ultimate Ying and yang.

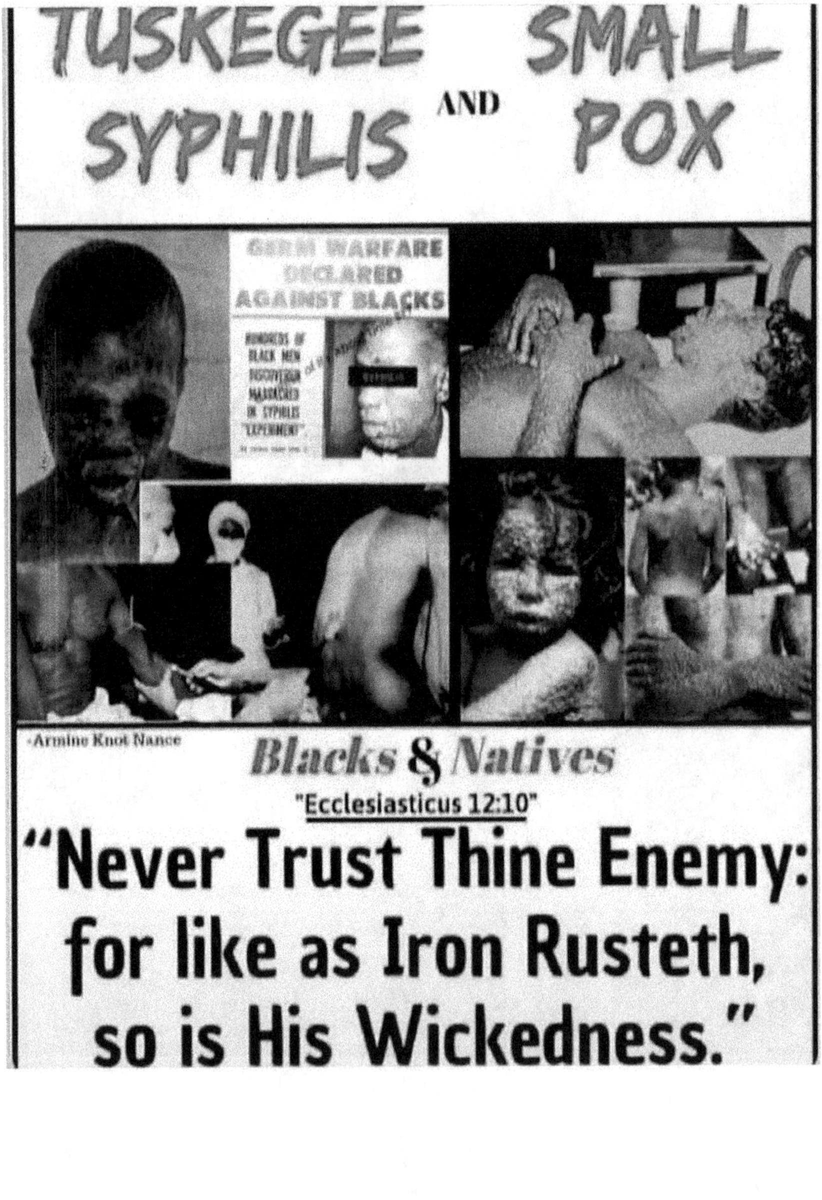
TUSKEGEE SYPHILIS
AND
SMALL POX
GERM WARFARE DECLARED AGAINST BLACKS
-Armine Knot Nance
Blacks & Natives
"Ecclesiasticus 12:10"
"Never Trust Thine Enemy: for like as Iron Rusteth, so is His Wickedness."

Chapter

5

Against all odds

"There is no language to
describe the horrors of Negro life in America."
James Baldwin

❧

The phrase "slavery was so long ago" is one phrase that makes my skin crawl and truly lets me know how uninformed a person is.

Yes, slavery in the United States "ended' a little over 150 years ago; however, we have been fighting pure evil ever since.

The Homestead Act

President Abraham Lincoln signed the original Homestead Act into law during the second year of the Civil War. Between 1868 and 1934, it granted 246 million acres of western land – an area close to the landmass of both California and Texas – to individual Americans, virtually for free. To receive 160 acres of government land, claimants had to complete a three-part process: first, file an application. Second, improve the land for five years. Third, file for the deed of ownership.

Shortly after emancipation in 1865, African Americans began fighting for the rights to the lands they had long worked – cultivated by their hands, fed by their sweat, and stained by their blood. Yet while the government stifled freedmen's demands for '40 acres and a mule' as just compensation for generations of unpaid, brutalized slave labor, they simultaneously granted free land to whites.

Indeed, when the failure of land distribution among native Black people during the Reconstruction is judged within the context of the Homestead Acts, the reality of the situation is laid bare. The problem was never the radical nature of land reform. The problem was racism.

With the advent of emancipation, therefore, native Black people became the only race in the US ever to start out, as an entire people, with close to zero capital. Having nothing else upon which to build or generate wealth, most freedmen had little real chance of breaking the cycles of poverty created by slavery and perpetuated by federal policy. The stain of slavery, it seems, is much more widespread and lasting than many Americans have admitted. Yet, it is the legacy of the Reconstruction – particularly the failure of land redistribution – that so closely coupled poverty and race in the US.

Slaveowners (Psychopathic criminals) got paid - We got zero

Red Lining

Redlining, a process by which banks and other institutions refuse to offer mortgages or offer worse rates to customers in certain neighborhoods based on their racial and ethnic composition, is one of the clearest examples of **institutionalized racism** in the history of the United States. Although the practice was formally outlawed in 1968 with the passage of the Fair Housing Act, it continues in various forms to this day.

History of Housing Discrimination

Fifty years after the abolition of enslavement, local governments continued to legally enforce housing segregation through **exclusionary zoning laws**, city ordinances that prohibited the sale of the property to Black people. In 1917 when the Supreme Court ruled these zoning laws unconstitutional, homeowners swiftly replaced them with **racially restrictive covenants**, agreements between property owners that banned the sale of homes in a neighborhood to certain racial groups.

By the time the Supreme Court found racially restrictive covenants themselves unconstitutional in 1947, the practice was so widespread that these agreements were difficult to invalidate and almost impossible to reverse. According to "Understanding Fair Housing," a document created by the U.S. Commission on Civil Rights, a 1937 magazine article reported that 80% of neighborhoods in Chicago and Los Angeles carried racially restrictive covenants by 1940.

The Federal Government Begins Redlining

The federal government was not involved in housing until 1934 when the Federal Housing Administration (FHA) was created as part of the New Deal. The FHA looked to restore the housing market after the Great Depression by incentivizing homeownership and introducing the mortgage lending system we still use today. Instead of creating policies to make housing fairer, the FHA did the opposite. It took advantage of racially restrictive covenants and insisted that the properties they insured use them. Along with the Homeowner's Loan Coalition (HOLC), a federally funded program created to help homeowners refinance their mortgages, the FHA introduced **redlining** policies in over 200 American cities.

Beginning in 1934, the HOLC included in the FHA Underwriting Handbook "residential security maps" used to help the government decide which neighborhoods would make secure investments and which should be off-limits for issuing mortgages. The maps were color-coded according to these guidelines:

- **Green ("Best"):** Green areas represented in-demand, up-and-coming neighborhoods where "professional men" lived. These neighborhoods were explicitly homogenous, lacking "a single foreigner or Negro."

- **Blue ("Still Desirable"):** These neighborhoods had "reached their peak" but were thought to be stable due to their low risk of "infiltration" by non-White groups.

- **Yellow ("Definitely Declining"):** Most yellow areas bordered Black neighborhoods. They were considered risky due to the "threat of infiltration of foreign-born, negro, or lower grade populations."

- **Red ("Hazardous"):** Red areas were neighborhoods where "infiltration" had already occurred. These neighborhoods, almost all of them populated by Black residents, were described by the HOLC as having an "undesirable population" and were ineligible for FHA backing.

These maps would help the government decide which properties were eligible for FHA backing. Green and blue neighborhoods, which usually had majority-White populations, were considered good investments. It was easy to get a loan in these areas. Yellow neighborhoods were considered "risky," and red areas (those with the highest percentage of Black residents) were ineligible for FHA backing.

The End of Redlining

The Fair Housing Act of 1968, which explicitly prohibited racial discrimination, put an end to legally sanctioned redlining policies like those used by the FHA. However, like racially restrictive covenants, redlining policies were difficult to stamp out and have continued even in recent years. A 2008 paper about predatory lending, for example, found denial rates for loans to Black people in Mississippi to be disproportionate compared to any racial discrepancy in credit score history.

In 2010, an investigation by the United States Justice Department found that the financial institution Wells Fargo had used similar policies to restrict loans to certain racial groups. The investigation began after a *New York Times* article exposed the company's own racially biased lending practices. The *Times* reported that loan officers had referred to their Black customers as "mud people" and to the subprime loans they pushed on them "ghetto loans."

Redlining policies are not limited to mortgage lending, however. Other industries also use race as a factor in their decision-making policies, usually in ways that ultimately hurt minorities. Some grocery stores, for example, have been shown to raise prices of certain products in stores found in primarily Black and Latino neighborhoods.

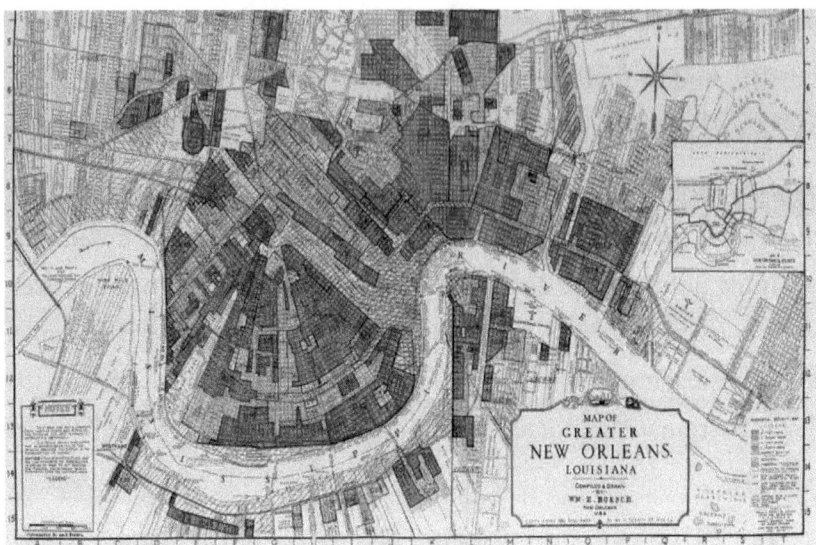

I remember hearing stories my mom would talk about when I was a toddler and she and my dad were a couple, she would have to pretend to be a single white woman, or no one would rent to her, and my dad would virtually have to sneak in and out the house to be with us.

The same country my dad's ancestors built for free, and he fought for in the Vietnam war he was not even welcome in – Make amends!

This was in the late 1970s ...not so long ago.

Jim Crow

Jim Crow laws were a collection of state and local statutes that legalized racial segregation. Named after a Black minstrel show character, the laws—which existed for about 100 years, from the post-Civil War era until 1968—were meant to marginalize African Americans by denying them the right to vote, hold jobs, get an education, or other opportunities. Those who tried to defy Jim Crow laws often faced arrest, fines, jail sentences, violence, and death.

Black Codes

The roots of Jim Crow laws began as early as 1865, immediately following the ratification of the 13th Amendment, which abolished slavery in the United States.

Black codes were strict local and state laws that detailed when, where, and how formerly enslaved people could work and for how much compensation. The codes appeared throughout the South as a legal way to put Black citizens into indentured servitude, to take voting rights away, to control where they lived and how they traveled, and to seize children for labor purposes.

The legal system was stacked against Black citizens, with former Confederate soldiers working as police and judges, making it difficult for African Americans to win court cases and ensuring they were subject to Black codes.

These codes worked in conjunction with labor camps for the incarcerated, where prisoners were treated as enslaved people. Black offenders typically received longer sentences than their white equals, and because of the grueling work, they often did not live out their entire sentence.

KKK

During the Reconstruction era, local governments, as well as the national Democratic Party and President Andrew Johnson, thwarted efforts to help Black Americans move forward.

Violence was on the rise, making danger a regular aspect of native black American life. Black schools were vandalized and destroyed, and bands of violent white people attacked, tortured, and lynched Black citizens in the night. Families were attacked and forced off their land all across the South.

The most ruthless organization of the Jim Crow era, the Ku Klux Klan, was born in 1865 in Pulaski, Tennessee, as a private club for Confederate veterans.

The KKK grew into a secret society terrorizing Black communities and seeping through white Southern culture, with members at the highest levels of government and in the lowest echelons of criminal back alleys.

Foundational black Americans have been fighting the epitome of evil since day one, hated, terrorized, and discriminated against for nothing more than the color of their skin- against all odds.

THIS PHOTO WAS TAKEN AT THE 1924 DEMOCRATIC NATIONAL CONVENTION

IT WAS KNOWN AS THE "KLANBAKE" (JUST IN CASE YOU WANT TO GOOGLE IT)

Comments

1wiffeymaterial My grandmother's (who I'm named after) grandmother was a slave .. One of the many reasons why back wages are owed!

27s   Reply

thestylinglounge_ My grandmom sister is still alive at 101 yr old. And she has all her senses still. She has so many different stories. One i never liked when her and her 12 siblings would be home and hear the kkk come thru their neighborhood and they had to turn off all their lights in the house and duck down until they passed by slowly on their horses.

2h   56 likes   Reply

Add a comment...   Post

And still, I rise:

Here are a few accounts of many where we were killed for absolutely nothing but being black and beating the odds.

Alberta Jones, first female black prosecutor thrown in Ohio river

Alberta O. Jones had a bright future in the law profession in Louisville, Kentucky. She was known as a trailblazer, creating a name for herself and breaking ground for women and Native black Americans in the legal world. She was the first black woman to pass the Kentucky bar exam and was the first female prosecutor in the state of Kentucky. But just five months after accepting the position, she was beaten and thrown in the Ohio River, where she died in August 1965.

Even though they had overwhelming fingerprint evidence and witnesses, no one was ever charged.

I WAS LOUISVILLE KENTUCKY FIRST BLACK FEMALE PROSECUTOR

@CONSCIOUS_BROTHA

BUT I WAS BEATEN MURDERED AND TOSSED INTO THE OHIO RIVER REMEMBER MY NAME ALBERTA ODELL JONES ESQUIRE

Lloyd Gaines

Lloyd Lionel Gaines (born 1911 – disappeared March 19, 1939) was the plaintiff in *Gaines v. Canada* (1938), one of the most important early court cases in the 20th-century U.S. civil rights movement. After being denied admission to the University of Missouri School of Law because he was African American and refusing the university's offer to pay for him to attend a neighboring state's law school that had no racial restriction, Gaines filed suit. The U.S. Supreme Court ultimately ruled in his favor, holding that the separate but equal doctrine required that Missouri either admit him or set up a separate law school for black students.

The Missouri General Assembly chose the latter option. It authorized the conversion of a former cosmetology school in St. Louis to establish the Lincoln University School of Law, to which other, mostly black, students were admitted. The National Association for the Advancement of Colored People (NAACP), which had supported Gaines's suit, planned to file another one challenging the adequacy of the new law school. While waiting for classes to begin, Gaines traveled between St. Louis, Kansas City, and Chicago, looking for work. He worked odd jobs and gave speeches before local NAACP chapters. One night in Chicago, he left the fraternity house, where he was staying, to buy stamps, and never returned. He was never seen again by anyone who knew or recognized him and reported doing so.

This is what you call blazing a trail.

Foundational black Americans have been making a way out of no way since the start of the America everyone wants to come to today.

We even built our own THRIVING communities, not just in Tulsa, but these communities were destroyed. So here is a shortlist of what was taken from us for no other reason than being black in America.

BLACK MASSACRES

Chicago•
1919

•Detroit
1943

New York•
1863

Springfield•
1908

Washington•
1919

•East St. Louis
1917

•Tulsa
1921

Memphis
1866

Wilmington•
1898

•Elaine
1919

•Atlanta
1906

•Charleston
2015

Vicksburg
1874

•Clinton
1875

Eufaula
1874

Slocum•
1910

Camila
1868

Colfax
1873

Rosewood•
1923

•Ocoee
1920

Opelousas
1868

St. Bernard Parish
1868

Thibadaux
1887

New Orleans
1866

Tulsa:

At the turn of the 20th century, Native black Americans founded and developed the Greenwood district in Tulsa, Oklahoma. Built on what had formerly been Indian Territory, the community grew and flourished as a Black economic and cultural mecca—until May 31, 1921.

That's when a white mob began a rampage through some 35 square blocks, decimating the community known proudly as "Black Wall Street." Armed rioters, many deputized by local police, looted and burned down businesses, homes, schools, churches, a hospital, hotel, public library, newspaper offices, and more. While the official death toll of the Tulsa race massacre was 36, historians estimate it may have been as high as 300. As many as 10,000 people were left homeless.

The incident stands as one most horrific acts of racial violence and domestic terrorism ever committed on American soil.

In May 2021, 100 years after the massacre, 107-year-old Viola Fletcher testified before Congress: "On May 31, of '21, I went to bed in my family's home in Greenwood," she recounted. "The neighborhood I fell asleep in that night was rich, not just in terms of wealth, but in culture…and heritage. My family had a beautiful home. We had great neighbors. I had friends to play with. I felt safe. I had everything a child could need. I had a bright future."

Then, she said, came the murderous rampage, still vivid in her mind 100 years later: "I still see Black men being shot, Black bodies lying in the street. I still smell smoke and see fire. I still see Black businesses being burned. I still hear airplanes flying overhead. I hear the screams." Make Amends

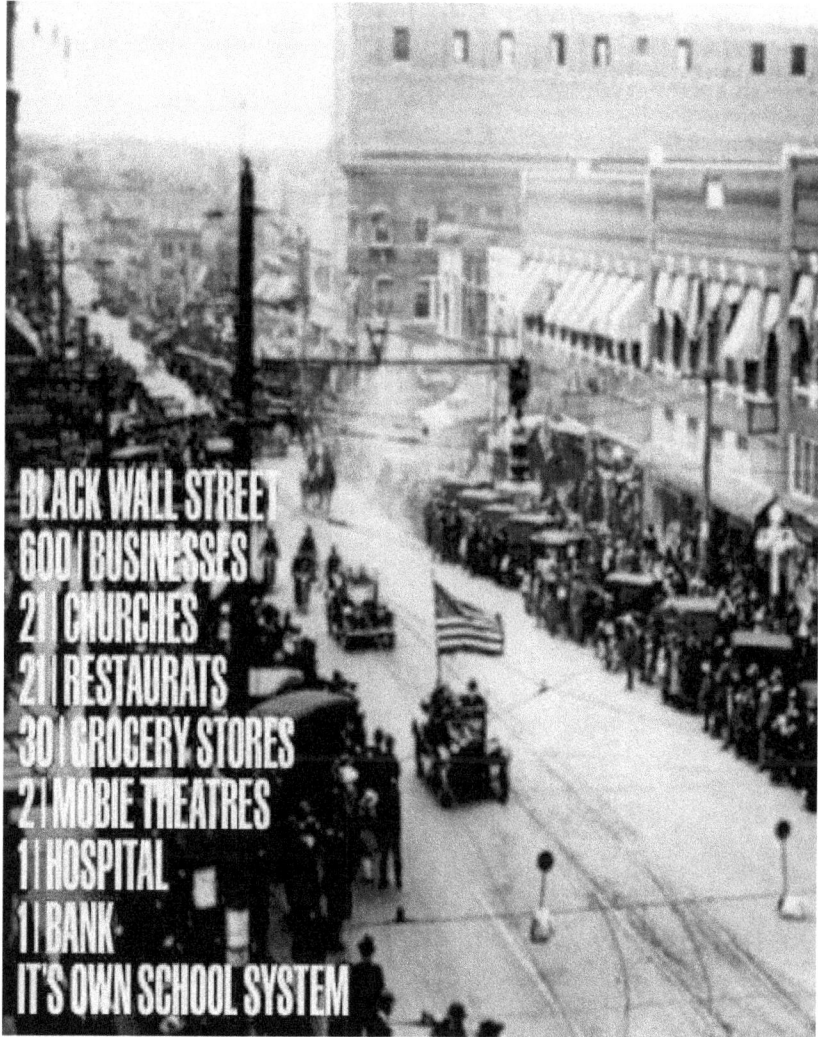

BLACK WALL STREET
600 | BUSINESSES
21 | CHURCHES
21 | RESTAURATS
30 | GROCERY STORES
2 | MOBIE THEATRES
1 | HOSPITAL
1 | BANK
IT'S OWN SCHOOL SYSTEM

Before they bombed black wall street.

Oscar Ville Ga – Lake Lanier

The very foundation of America stands on misrepresentations and down-right lies about American history, especially history associated with the plight of Native Black people and acts of racism in America. One must ask, why? What are the skeletons hiding beneath the surface of American history? Why are the authors of American history not telling the truth? Such is the history of Lake Lanier.

Just a very short 42 miles north of Atlanta beneath a lake lies the truth of a small village called Oscarville, Georgia. It was a thriving village that was predominantly Black owned. Why is a village beneath a lake, you ask? Welp, 108 years ago, an incident changed the lives of 1,098 Black families forever. Make Amends

Seneca Village, Central Park

Central Park is the most visited urban park in the United States, receiving approximately 37.5 million visitors annually. However, what many visitors don't know is that a portion of the park was once home to a thriving Black community in the 1800s.

Before the city built Central Park, the area from West 82nd to West 89th streets and between 7th and 8th avenues was the location of what was known as Seneca Village, a predominantly Native black American community that included the largest group of Native black property owners in New York at that time. The village existed from 1825 to 1857.

"Seneca Village had approximately 50 homes, three churches and one school. A local spring supplied fresh water, and there is some evidence that residents had gardens and raised livestock," said Central Park Conservancy's historian, Marie Warsh. "Approximately half of the Native Black population in Seneca Village owned their homes, making it the largest community of Native black property owners in 19th century New York City."

In 1825, John and Elizabeth Whitehead began selling pieces of their farmland. A young Native black American man named Andrew Williams bought the first three lots for $125. Two dozen plots were sold to members of the Black Methodist Episcopal Zion Church, which was the largest and wealthiest Black church community in the country.

In 1857, with plans to create an urban park in Manhattan, the state of New York used eminent domain to evict residents and buy the land. The community was never moved or re-established.

"The creation of Central Park resulted in the dissolution of Seneca Village," Warsh said. "To create Central Park, the New York State Legislature authorized the use of eminent domain, the power of a government to take private land for public use, with compensation paid to the landowner. This was common practice in 19th century urban America, and a similar use of eminent domain had been used to build Manhattan's grid of streets decades earlier."

The Elaine Massacre:

The Elaine Massacre was by far the deadliest racial confrontation in Arkansas history and possibly the bloodiest racial conflict in the history of the United States. While its deepest roots lay in the state's commitment to white supremacy, the events in Elaine (Phillips County) stemmed from tense race relations and growing concerns about labor unions. A shooting incident that occurred at a meeting of the Progressive Farmers and Household Union escalated into mob violence on the part of the white people in Elaine and surrounding areas. Although the exact number is unknown, estimates of the number of Native black Americans killed by whites' range into the hundreds; five white people lost their lives.

The conflict began on the night of September 30, 1919, when approximately 100 Native Black Americans, mostly sharecroppers on the plantations of white landowners, attended a meeting of the Progressive Farmers and Household Union of America at a church in Hoop Spur (Phillips County), three miles north of Elaine. The purpose of the meeting, one of several by black sharecroppers in the Elaine area during the previous months, was to obtain better payments for their cotton crops from the white plantation owners who dominated the area during the Jim Crow era. Black sharecroppers were often exploited in their efforts to collect payment for their cotton crops.

Orangeburg Massacre:

The Orangeburg Massacre occurred on the night of February 8, 1968, when a civil rights protest at South Carolina State University (SC State) turned deadly after highway patrol officers opened fire on about 200 unarmed black student protestors. Three young men were shot and killed, and 28 people were wounded. The event became known as the Orangeburg Massacre and is one of the most violent episodes of the civil rights movement, yet it is still one of the least recognized.

Rosewood Massacre:

The Rosewood Massacre was an attack on the predominantly Native Black American town of Rosewood, Florida, in 1923 by large groups of white aggressors. The town was entirely destroyed by the end of the violence, and the residents were driven out permanently. The story was mostly forgotten until the 1980s when it was revived and brought to public attention.

Rosewood, Florida

Though it was originally settled in 1845 by both Black and white people, black codes and Jim Crow laws in the years after the Civil War fostered segregation in Rosewood (and much of the South).

Employment was provided by pencil factories, but the cedar tree population soon became decimated, and white families moved away in the 1890s and settled in the nearby town of Sumner.

By the 1920s, Rosewood's population of about 200 was entirely made up of Black citizens, except for one white family that ran the general store there.

Ocoee

The Ocoee massacre considered the "single bloodiest day in modern American political history," was a violent race riot that broke out on November 2, 1920. All this happened because black citizens wanted to vote. Native black-American-owned buildings and residences in northern Ocoee, a city in Orange County, Florida, were burned to the ground. The Native black Americans residing in Ocoee who were not direct victims of the race riot were later driven out by threats or force. A total of 330 acres plus 48 city lots owned by 18 Black families living in Ocoee, Florida, were lost. In 2001, the land lost by the 18 Ocoee families, not including buildings now on it, is assessed by tax officials at more than $4.2 million, according to the AP report. Ocoee would then become an all-white town and remain as such "until sixty-one years later in 1981."

Ocoee was founded in the 1850s as a camp for laborers working the farms around the southern shores of Lake Apopka. By 1920 there were just over 1,000 residents; almost half of them were Native black Americans. Two distinct Black communities developed in Ocoee. The southern Black community—known locally as the Baptist Quarters—sprung up around the Friendship Baptist Church, founded in 1896. The northern Black community, commonly known as the Methodist Quarters. Its namesake, Ocoee African Methodist Episcopal Church, held its first service in 1890.

The Ocoee Massacre, on election day 1920 over 50 to 60 African Americans were killed when one African American man attempted to vote.

Slocum,

The Slocum Massacre occurred on July 29, 1910, in Slocum, Texas, an unincorporated community in southeast Anderson County. The city used to be home to a thriving Native Black American community with several businesses and farms owned by black residents.

Leading up to the massacre, the lynching of a black man in nearby Cherokee County sparked racial tensions in the Slocum area. While rumors circulated that black residents had been meeting in Slocum to plan an armed rebellion. Racial tensions only intensified when a white man reportedly sought to collect a disputed debt from a well-respected black farmer named Abe Wilson and when a road construction foreman put a Native Black American in charge of soliciting aid for road improvements. A confrontation erupted, enraging Jim Spurger, a local white farmer, who became the primary agitator of the conflict that led to the massacre. Many newspapers and eyewitness accounts reported that Spurger instigated the events by claiming that Black people had threatened him.

Polk County,

On Aug. 5, 1896, white workers attacked Black workers in Arkansas who were coming to work on the Kansas City, Pittsburg, and Gulf Railway.

As a result, three Native Black Americans were killed and eight wounded. Although reports place some of the events near Horatio, accounts clearly said that the purpose of the attack was to keep Native black Americans out of Polk County, and so it was generally referred to as the Polk County Race War.

This was part of a pattern of labor-related racial terrorism that was sweeping Arkansas at the time

Thibodaux,

On November 23, 1887, white vigilantes gunned down unarmed black laborers and their families during a spree lasting more than two hours. The violence erupted due to strikes on Louisiana sugar cane plantations. Fear, rumor, and white supremacist ideals clashed with an unprecedented labor action to create an epic tragedy. A future member of the U.S. House of Representatives was among the leaders of a mob that routed black men from houses and forced them to a stretch of railroad track, ordering them to run for their lives before gunning them down. According to a witness, the guns firing in the black neighborhoods sounded like a battle.

Hamburg Massacre,

The Hamburg Massacre was a riot in the American town of Hamburg, South Carolina, in July 1876, leading up to the last election season of the Reconstruction Era. It was the first of a series of civil disturbances planned and conducted by white Democrats in the majority-black Republican Edgefield District to suppress black Americans' civil rights and voting rights and disrupt Republican meetings through actual and threatened violence.

Sundown towns:

Sundown Towns are all-white communities, neighborhoods, or counties that exclude Black people and other minorities through discriminatory laws, harassment, and threats or use of violence. The name derives from the posted and verbal warnings issued to Black people that although they might be allowed to work or travel in a community during the daytime, they must leave by sundown. Although the term most often refers to the forced exclusion of Black people, the history of sundown towns also includes prohibitions against Jews, Native Americans, Chinese, Japanese, and other minority groups.

Although it is difficult to make a correct count, historians estimate there were up to 10,000 sundown towns in the United States between 1890 and 1960, mostly in the Mid-West and West. They began to proliferate during the Great Migration, starting in about 1910, when large numbers of Native black Americans left the South to escape racism and poverty. As Black people began to migrate to other regions of the country, many predominantly white communities actively discouraged them from settling there.

The Devils Punchbowl:

There is a closely guarded secret that has been deliberately buried by mainstream media and historians: After the Civil War (and during the war), millions of freed Black people were funneled into concentration camps in America and killed through **forced starvation** and other means.

Many of these locations were called "contraband camps," and they were hastily built internment camps that were generally in proximity to Union army camps.

One gruesome camp, in particular, was located in **Natchez. Ms**. The Devil's Punchbowl is a place found in Natchez, where during the Civil War, authorities forced tens of thousands of freed slaves to live in these American death camps. Researcher Paula Westbrook said, "The union army did not allow them to remove the bodies from the camp. They just gave 'em shovels and said bury 'em where they drop."

"When the slaves were released from the plantations during the occupation, they overran Natchez. And the population went from about 10,000 to 120,000 overnight," Westbrook said.

"So, they decided to build an encampment for 'em at Devil's Punchbowl, which they walled off and wouldn't let 'em out," Don Estes, former director of the Natchez City Cemetery, said.

In Natchez, Mississippi alone, officials estimate that in the time span of just one year, over 20,000 free Black people were killed in the concentration camp.

Devil's Punch Bowl - US Concentration Camp Where Thousands Died Has Been Erased from History

● History

Historians concerned about the fate of African-Americans in the immediate aftermath of the Civil War are working to piece together the story of the Devil's Punchbowl, a hellish concentration camp in Natchez in Mississippi which might be one of the most disturbing incidents in all of American history.

Weeksville:

Weeksville was named after **James Weeks**, a Native Black American stevedore from Virginia. In 1838 (11 years after the final abolition of slavery in New York State), Weeks bought a plot of land from Henry C. Thompson, a free Native Black American and land investor, in the Ninth Ward of central Brooklyn. Thompson had acquired the land from Edward Copeland, a politically minded European American and Brooklyn grocer, in 1835. Previously Copeland bought the land from an heir of John Lefferts, a member of one of the most prominent and land-holding families in Brooklyn. There was ample opportunity for land acquisition during this time, as many prominent land-holding families sold off their properties during an intense era of land speculation. Many Native black Americans saw land acquisition as their opportunity to gain economic and political freedom by building their own communities. The NYC Parks website confuses Weeks with a man of the same name who lived 1776-1863.

The village itself was established by a group of Native Black American land investors and political activists. It covered an area in the borough's eastern Bedford Hills area, bounded by present-day Fulton Street, East New York Avenue, Ralph Avenue, and Troy Avenue. A 1906 article in the *New York Age* recalling the earlier period noted that James Weeks "owned a handsome dwelling at Schenectady and Atlantic Avenues."

By the 1850s, Weeksville had more than 500 residents from all over the East Coast (as well as two people born in Africa). Almost 40 percent of residents were southern born. Nearly one-third of the men over 21 owned land; in antebellum New York, unlike in New England, non-white men had to own real property (to the value of $250) and pay taxes on it to qualify as voters. The village had its own churches (including Bethel Tabernacle African Methodist Episcopal Church and the Berean Missionary Baptist Church), a school ("Colored School no. 2", now P.S. 243), a cemetery, and an old age home. Weeksville had one of the first Native Black newspapers, the *Freedman's Torchlight*, and in the 1860s became the national headquarters of the African Civilization Society and the Howard Colored Orphan Asylum. In addition, the Colored School was the first such school in the U.S. to integrate both its staff and its students.

During the violent New York Draft Riots of 1863, the community served as a refuge for many African-Americans who fled from Manhattan.

After completing the Brooklyn Bridge and as New York City grew and expanded, Weeksville gradually became part of Crown Heights, and memory of the village was largely forgotten.

Even when we made something of ourselves or built our own communities – we were destroyed – make amends

DEADLIEST MASS SHOOTINGS* IN US HISTORY

- Greenwood, OK – 1921
  – Up to 3000 Black killed
- East St. Louis, IL – 1917
  – Up to 700 Blacks killed
- Ft. Pillow, TN – 1864
  – Up to 300 Blacks killed
- Thibodeaux, LA – 1887
  – up to 300 Blacks killed
- Ft. Negro, FL – 1817
  – Up to 270 Blacks killed
- New Orleans, LA – 1866
  – Up to 200 Blacks killed
- Opelousas, LA – 1868
  – Up to 200 Blacks killed

- Slocum / Palestine, TX – 1910
  – Up to 200 Blacks killed
- New York, NY – 1741
  – Up to 152 Blacks killed
- Colfax, LA – 1873
  – Up to 150 Blacks killed
- Rosewood, FL – 1923
  – At least 150 Blacks killed
- New York, NY [Draft Riots] – 1863
  – Up to 120 Blacks killed
- Elaine, AR – 1919
  – Up to 100 Blacks killed

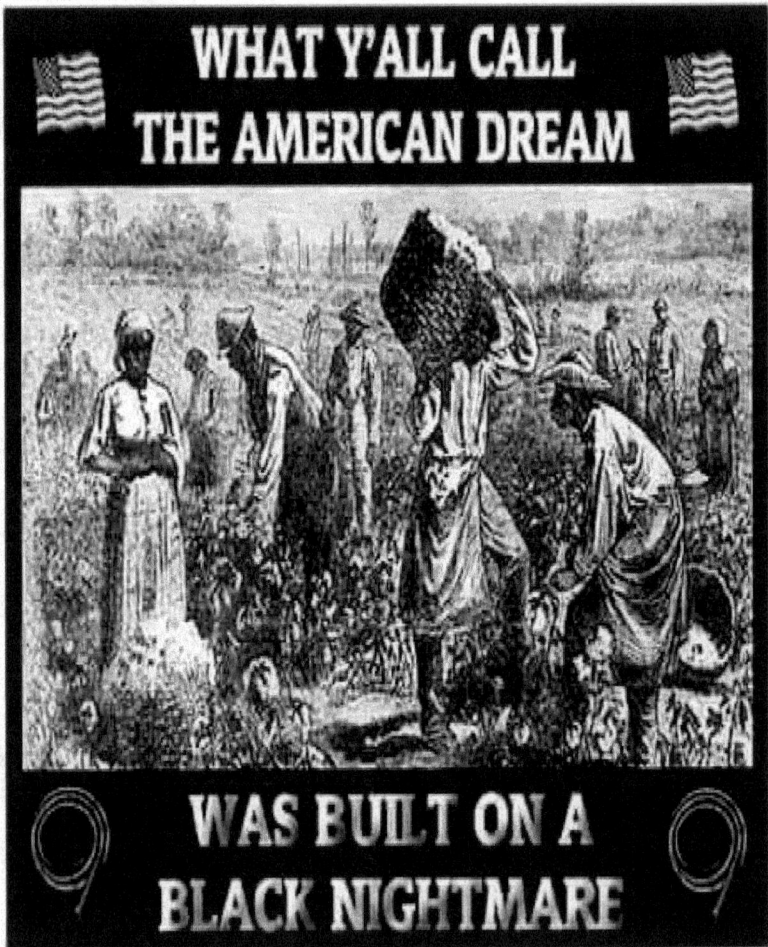

Make Amends

Chapter

6

The Fight continues

❧

"And still, I RISE"

Recap where we are on History:

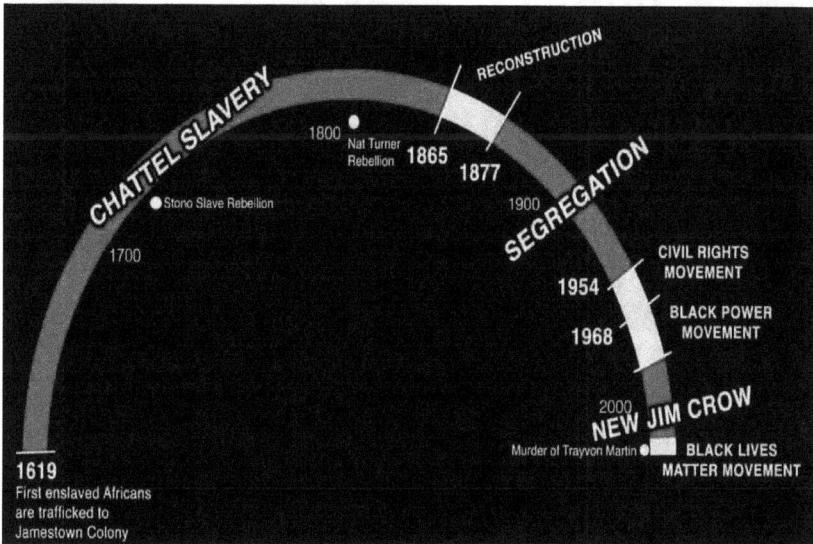

Eugenics

I am not going to go into too much depth on Eugenics, as I plan on offering a class on this subject.

So, this will just be a quick overview.

Eugenics is a set of beliefs and practices that aim to improve the genetic quality of a human population, historically by excluding people and groups judged to be inferior or promoting those judged to be superior.

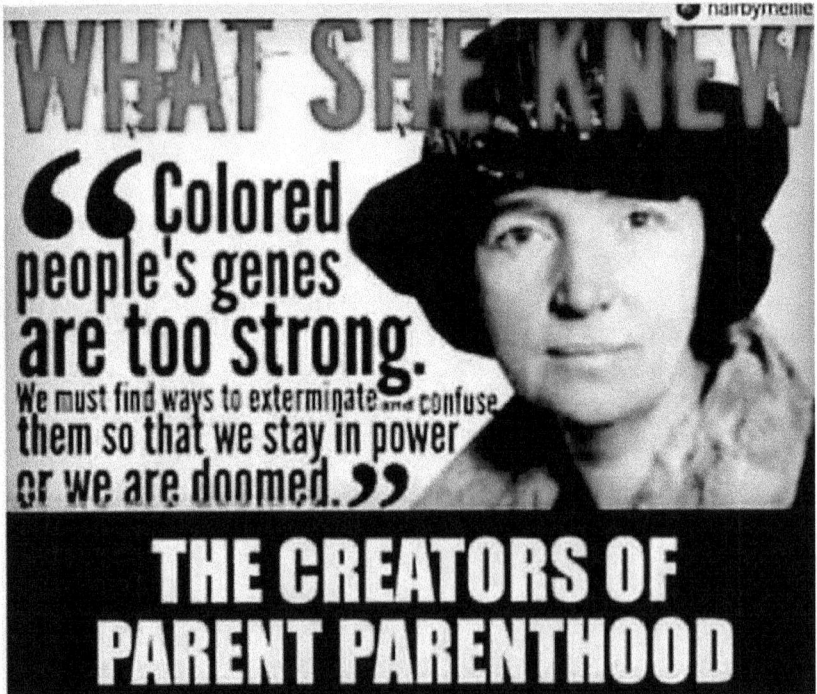

Bill Gates' father, William H. Gates, Sr., served on the board of Planned Parenthood (PP) during the group's infancy — a re-branded organization birthed out of the American Eugenics Society.

Make no mistake: Planned Parenthood was built on population control schemes, allied with the same groups who wanted genetic hierarchy laws to 'preserve' humanity and looked to 'beautify' countries by stopping the "unfit" from reproducing.

DID YOU KNOW???

That when blacks started uniting to peacefully protest in 60's & 70's, Hoover sent FBI agents to infiltrate the movements, loot, incite riots and commit other acts of violence. The program is called Cointelpro.

Cointelpro/ Dismantling of the black panthers and cause dissent in anything challenging the current rule of white supremacy.

COINTELPRO was a counterintelligence program run by the Federal Bureau of Investigation (FBI) from roughly 1956 to 1976. It combined the efforts of the Bureau and local police forces to track, harass, discredit, infiltrate, destroy, and destabilize dissident groups in the United States. COINTELPRO targeted the Communist Party, the Socialist Workers Party, the American Indian Movement, those considered part of the "New Left," the KKK, and most acutely, black civil rights and militant black nationalist groups.

J. Edgar Hoover, the director of the FBI, considered militant black nationalist groups to be the most dangerous threat facing the United States at that time due to their perceived potential to cause civil unrest and violence. The FBI's COINTELPRO focused on the Black Panther Party, Malcolm X, the Nation of Islam, and others. COINTELPRO also looked to undermine, intimidate, and slander avowedly nonviolent black leaders such as Martin Luther King Jr.

The counterintelligence methods used by the FBI program included sending undercover agents into the Black Panther Party, where they incited criminal acts and fomented much of the violence that the public came to negatively associate with the Panthers. Other methods included planting informants, video surveillance, wiretapping, and phone call campaigns and false letter writing to sow intragroup discord. Indeed, COINTELPRO is suspected of having contributed to the divide between Malcolm X and the Nation of Islam that resulted in his assassination in 1965.

The FBI actively sabotaged and dismantled the American Indian Movement, the Chicano Movement, and the Black Power movement but the KKK is still alive and well today.

On December 4, 1969, Chicago police, in conjunction with the FBI, murdered 21-year-old Chairman Fred Hampton as he slept with his pregnant fiancée.

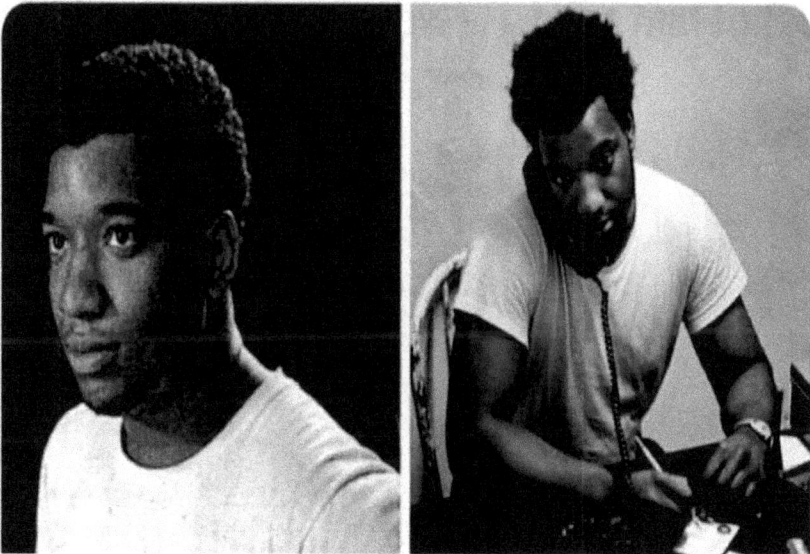

LONG LIVE Lil' Bobby Hutton, one of the original founders/first recruit of The Black Panther Party. After being bombed w/ tear gas & trapped in a burning basement, ^{KWR} Bobby Hutton came out shirtless to show he was unarmed & the police immediately shot him dead. He was only 17 years old...

The popo (police)

Growing up in Los Angeles in the late 1970s and 80s and 90s, I/ we never considered the police our friends or someone to protect us. It was actually quite the opposite—whenever I saw the police, I felt nothing but fear—even as a child.

So, to have seen the news highlight of the obvious genocide of black people lately does not come as a surprise to me at all.

Yes, the news unfairly reports on how many people the police kill, black and white and otherwise.

But also, yes, black people are seen as criminals from an early age due to the programming we are intentionally fed.

So, I would be remiss not to mention some of the lives needlessly lost at the hands of those supposed to be paid to protect us.

Foundational black Americans have been on their own and still are when it comes to protecting ourselves from hatred.

Kendrick Johnson's body was discovered at Lowndes High School in Valdosta, Ga., in January 2013. The 17-year-old disappeared one afternoon and was found the next morning with his head facing down inside an upright rolled-up gym mat and his feet sticking out of the top.

State authorities ruled his death an accident in 2013, suggesting he dove into the mat to retrieve a shoe and got trapped inside after an autopsy found that he died of «positional asphyxia.» The Lowndes County Sheriff's Office closed the case

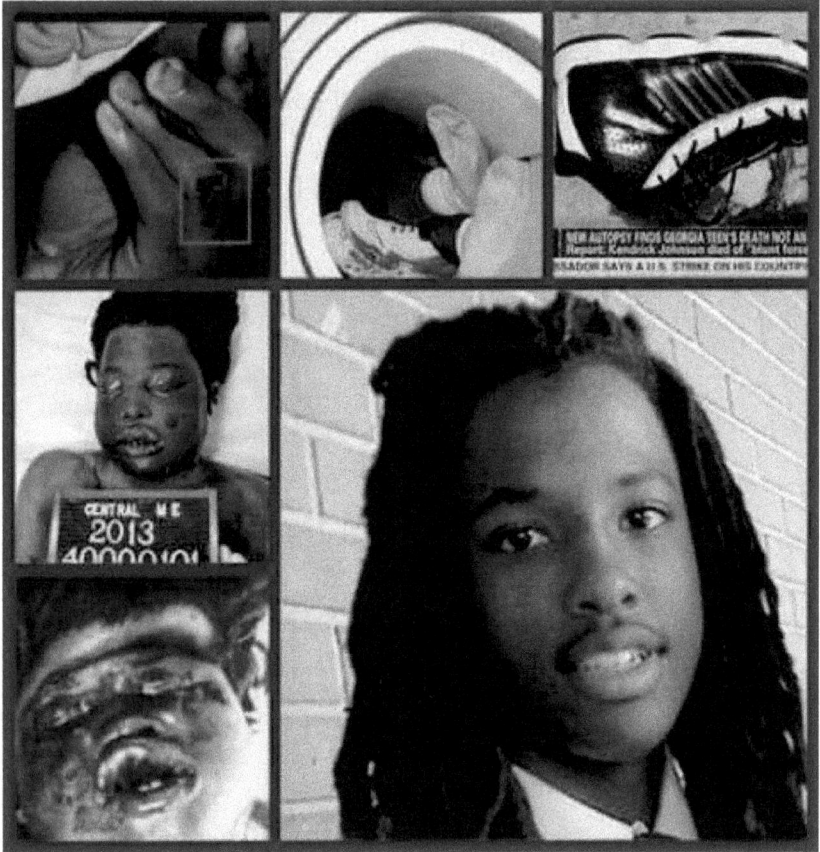

89 Lynchings Of Black Men In The Past 5 Years

Lynching Has Never

Jermaine
Carter
-2010
Mississippi

Stoped -The

Law Call's It Suicide Now!

Malcom Harsch   Robert Fuller

Two black men were found hanged to death in
public places in Victorville, CA and then Palmdale,
CA 50 miles apart, ten days apart, and local
authorities are saying both deaths were suicides.

**They are going to need some exceptional
evidence to back those claims up.**

The fight is far from over.

Chapter:

7

Other notable unsung heroes

"Some of us are chained; none of us are free."

❧

Before I even start this section, I want to clarify white privilege does not mean you somehow had it easier or didn't have to work and struggle for everything you've got- it only means that your skin color was not an obstacle for you.

IF I HEAR ONE MORE WHITE PERSON SAY THEY AREN'T PRIVILEGED BC THEY GREW UP POOR, I'M GONNA LOOSE MY MIND.

WHITE PRIVILEGE ISN'T ABOUT NOT HAVING MONEY. IT'S NOT ABOUT GROWING UP POOR. IT'S ABOUT BEING ABLE TO WALK DOWN THE STREET AND NOT BE STARED AT. IT'S ABOUT WALKING IN A STORE AND NOT BEING FOLLOWED BC THEY THINK YOU ARE GOING TO STEAL. WHITE PRIVILEGE IS ABOUT NOT BEING TARGETED. WHITE PRIVILEGE HAS NOTHING TO DO WITH THE AMOUNT OF MONEY YOU HAVE. IT HAS EVERYTHING TO DO WITH HOW THE COLOR OF YOUR SKIN HAS NEVER NEGATIVELY AFFECTED YOUR LIFE.

White allies

White people are not the enemy of black people, as we have always had white allies help in the struggle – it is the evil rich and powerful who are the true enemy; history itself proves this statement.

Now before anyone says, "well, you're half white," let me let you in on a little of my background and history. Biologically, I am half white, but the only family I have ever known is black.

The story goes: my mom's side of the family (the white side) disowned her when she was pregnant with me. So, I have never, ever even met anyone from that side my whole life, and to be honest, I have never trusted white people my whole life because of this story I was told.

I had a strong dislike for most white people because I have never known any too closely besides my brother-in-law and his family, who are not racist.

It took deep thought, a study of history, and being self-educated to look at things rationally and objectively to understand how they (the rich and powerful) have a strong vested interest in keeping us divided for superficial reasons.

Timmy, who works at CVS (the average white guy), is not the enemy to black people. He is just trying to etch out a living like most people, and frankly, doesn't owe anyone anything. His bloodline was not rich, so he had to work for everything he owns as well; the only difference is he hasn't been systematically destroyed (but helped), nor has his skin color ever been an obstacle. Neither of these are his fault or his doing. Being born white does not mean he is out to destroy black people or owes anyone anything. The people who owe Foundational Black Americans are the government and the ultra-rich who directly profited off our free labor, no one else owes us anything monetarily.

But everyone does owe us a thank you and a deep respect for our sacrifices.

In fact, however, white Americans are owed a thank you as well because they have helped us in the struggle to get America to the place it is in now—the greatest country on earth.

Can you imagine if tomorrow the United States enforced a law that all Asian people would be slaves in the South like Foundational Black Americans once were, but if they could only get to the North, they would be free? Now, of course, if you were Asian, you would most likely feel a duty and have a vested interest in helping your people. But who else would help? Would black people risk their own ass to help hide Asian people on the run to the free north just because it's the right thing to do? Even putting your own family at risk?

I believe a lot would and a lot wouldn't – myself personally would never put my children at risk to help strangers- but this is exactly what a lot of white Americans did to help us along the under-ground railroad- totally bucking the fugitive slave act and fighting against it, breaking the law, and risking their own family and livelihood.

Yes, there was a time in American History that the government made it legal to hunt real live people down like animals and return them to their owner- and if anyone even tried to help these runaway

Foundational Black American prisoners of war – they would be treated like criminals themselves.

In 1850, Congress passed the controversial Fugitive Slave Act, which required all escaped enslaved people to be returned to their owners and American citizens to cooperate with the captures.

So, lets bring this to modern day times, would you hide people running away from unjust laws, risking yourself and your family in the process by breaking these laws yourself?

CAUTION!!

COLORED PEOPLE

OF BOSTON, ONE & ALL,

You are hereby respectfully CAUTIONED and advised, to avoid conversing with the

Watchmen and Police Officers of Boston,

For since the recent ORDER OF THE MAYOR & ALDERMEN, they are empowered to act as

KIDNAPPERS

AND

Slave Catchers,

And they have already been actually employed in KIDNAPPING, CATCHING, AND KEEPING SLAVES. Therefore, if you value your LIBERTY, and the *Welfare of the Fugitives* among you, *Shun* them in every possible manner, as so many *HOUNDS* on the track of the most unfortunate of your race.

Keep a Sharp Look Out for KIDNAPPERS, and have TOP EYE open.

APRIL 24, 1851.

$100 REWARD.

Ranaway from the subscriber's farm, near Washington, on the 11th of October, negro woman SOPHIA GORDON, about 24 years of age, rather small in size, of copper color, is tolerably good looking, has a low and soft manner of speech. She is believed to be among associates formed in Washington where she has been often hired.

I will give the above reward, no matter where taken and secured in jail so that I get her again.

GEORGE W. YOUNG.

November 16th, 1856.

It was **against the law** to help, but many white Americans didn't care; they helped anyway for the only reason that it was the right thing to do. On behalf of them, you're welcome.

The abolitionist movement was an organized effort to end the practice of slavery in the United States. The first leaders of the campaign, from about 1830 to 1870, mimicked some of the same tactics British abolitionists had used to end slavery in Great Britain in the 1830s. Though it started as a movement with religious underpinnings, abolitionism became a controversial political issue that divided much of the country. Supporters and critics often engaged in heated debates and violent — even deadly — confrontations. The divisiveness and animosity fueled by the movement, along with other factors, led to the Civil War and, ultimately, the end of slavery.

As the name implies, an abolitionist is a person who looked to abolish slavery during the 19th century. More specifically, these individuals looked for the immediate and full emancipation of all enslaved people.

Most early abolitionists were white, religious Americans, but some of the most prominent leaders of the movement were also Black men and women who had escaped from bondage.

The abolitionists saw slavery as an abomination and an affliction on the United States, making it their goal to eradicate slave ownership. They sent petitions to Congress, ran for political office, and inundated people of the South with anti-slavery literature.

One of the most famous but unsung white American heroes, in my opinion, is John Brown.

John Brown holds a unique place in American history, often viewed as a force for good and an evil man at the same time.

Brown was a revolutionary abolitionist in the United States who became famous in his own time for practicing armed insurrection as a means to abolish slavery for good. He led the Pottawatomie Massacre, during which five men were killed in 1856 in Bleeding Kansas and became notorious for his attempted raid at Harpers Ferry in 1859. For that, he was tried and executed for treason against the state of Virginia, for murder, and conspiracy. Brown has been called "the most controversial of all 19th-century Americans." Brown's attempt in 1859 to start a liberation movement among enslaved Foundation Native Black Americans in Harpers Ferry, Virginia (now West Virginia) electrified the nation. He was tried for treason against the state of Virginia, the murder of five pro-slavery Southerners, and inciting a slave insurrection and was subsequently hanged. Southerners alleged that his rebellion was the tip of the abolitionist iceberg and stood for the wishes of the Republican Party to end slavery. Historians agree that the Harpers Ferry raid in 1859 escalated tensions that, a year later, led to secession and the Civil War. Brown's final speech, his interview in prison, and the final note he wrote the day he was executed predicted that slavery would only be abolished through the spilling of blood.

Who was John Brown?

- Revolutionary Abolitionist
- Was born may 9, 1800
- Died December 2, 1859
- He led small groups during the bleeding Kansas crisis
- He led 21 men on a raid of the federal arsenal at Harpers Ferry, Virginia(also known as John Brown's Raid)
- He had a very passionately religious family.

TREASON !

All TRUE CHRISTIANS who believe in " Immortality through Jesus Christ alone," are requested to pray for

CAPT. JOHN BROWN,

who now is under sentence of death, and is to be hung next month for righteousness sake, and doing justly with his fellow man, his country and his God.

By request of one who loves the Truth, and feels for the man that is to die a martyr to it.   J.

Somersworth, Nov. 4, 1859.

The first American hung for treason was a white American man fighting for Foundational Black Americans to be free. Thank you

Treason:

the crime of betraying one's country, especially by attempting to kill the sovereign or overthrow the government.

It was the law to keep foundational black Americans enslaved. Yet, many white allies broke the law to help black people for no other reason but to stand on their own convictions and morals.

The Freedom Riders challenged this status quo by riding interstate buses in the South in mixed racial groups to challenge local laws or customs that enforced segregation in seating. The Freedom Rides, and the violent reactions they provoked, bolstered the credibility of the American Civil Rights Movement. They called national attention to the disregard for the federal law and the local violence used to enforce segregation in the southern United States. Police arrested riders for trespassing, unlawful assembly, violating state and local Jim Crow laws, and other alleged offenses, but often they first let white mobs attack them without intervention.

A lot of White Americans have always fought for what is right for everyone in America since its inception, so it behooves us all to recognize any propaganda that tells us this is a black vs. white problem is only something they push to keep us arguing and divided, which only hurts us, the average American.

"Shout out to all my white brothers and sisters that are the descendants of abolitionists and use their privilege to empower the oppressed"

White Panther Party

The White Panthers were an anti-racist political collective founded in November 1968 by Pun Plamondon, Leni Sinclair, and John Sinclair. It was started in response to an interview where Huey P. Newton, co-founder of the Black Panther Party, was asked what white people could do to support the Black Panthers.

the White Panthers

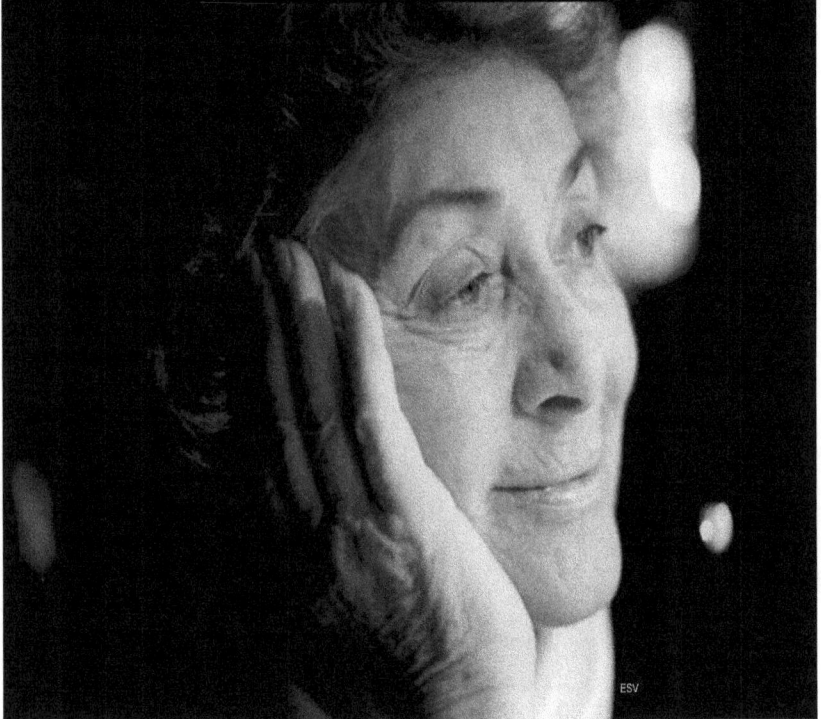

Silence in the face of injustice is complicity with the oppressor.
Ginetta Sagan

Chicanos

❧

The only other group that has any kind of rightful claim to America would be Mexicans, and in my opinion, Chicanos specifically.

Most land out west belonged to Mexico before the Mexican American War (1846-1848) marked the first U.S. armed conflict chiefly fought on foreign soil. It pitted a politically divided and militarily unprepared Mexico against the expansionist-minded administration of U.S. President James K. Polk, who believed the United States had a "manifest destiny" to spread across the continent to the Pacific Ocean. A border skirmish along the Rio Grande started off the fighting and was followed by a series of U.S. victories. When the dust cleared, Mexico had lost about one-third of its territory, including nearly all present-day California, Utah, Nevada, Arizona, and New Mexico.

But what about the people who have been on that said land for centuries?

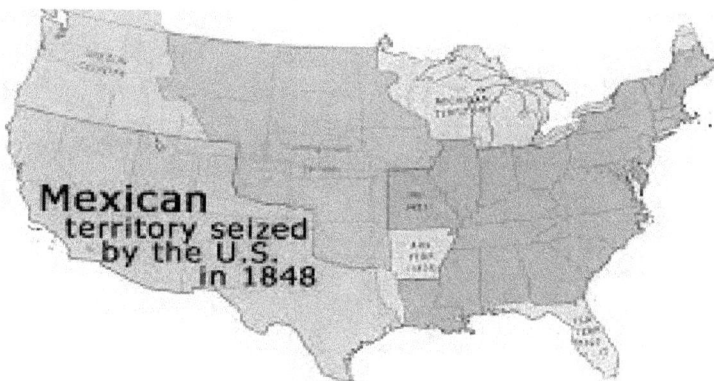

Another reason I want to thank Mexican Americans is for the food; I am not kidding!

Everyone loves nachos, tacos, burritos, tortas, enchiladas, tamales, and anything else resembling Mexican cuisine.

From Tequila to Corona to Modelo to margaritas, Mexican cuisine dominates the Latin American food scene – and it's delicious!

Lastly, Mexico is one of the top destination vacation spots in the world, everyone loves Mexican beaches – Thank you!

aboriginal_willie

Mexican Aboriginal La escuela en Pueblos Indios

See Translation

Haiti

❦

Haitian Revolution (1791-1804), a series of conflicts between Haitian slaves, colonists, the armies of the British and French colonizers, and several other parties. Through the struggle, the Haitian people ultimately won independence from France and thereby became the first country to be founded by former slaves.

The first slave colony to fight off its captors.

Many aren't aware that without Haiti's help, many countries in Latin America would not have obtained their independence. Simon Bolivar arrived in Haiti in December 1815, downtrodden and accompanied by Venezuelan families and soldiers after being badly trampled by the Spaniards in Cartagena. Bolivar was attempting to free South American countries, which are now Venezuela, Colombia, Peru, Chile, modern Bolivia.

President Pétion was the President of Haiti, and he helped Bolivar. When they were leaving the island in December 1816, the President gave him not only supplies but Haitian soldiers—about 300 of them. Bolivar's fight was not easy, it was rather very difficult, but ultimately, he successfully obtained the independence of modern-day north-west Brazil, Guyana, Venezuela, Ecuador, Colombia, Panama, northern Peru, Costa Rica, Nicaragua, and Bolivia. As promised to Pétion, Simon Bolivar abolished slavery in those territories. The agreement between President Pétion and Bolivar was kept secret because Haiti's assistance would have been considered an act of war by the U.S. and Spain.

Dear media, if you insist on starting EVERY article about Haiti with "the poorest country in the Western Hemisphere" respectfully add "first independent black nation in the western hemisphere, first post-colonial independence black led nation in the world and the only nation whose independence was gained as part of a successful slave rebellion.

Thank you!

Jamaica

———
❧

No one has serenaded the world like Foundational Native black Americans, but the only other genre of music that comes close to our worldwide appeal is Reggae.

And one cannot mention Reggae without mentioning Bob Marley, a top freedom fighter through his music that could never be duplicated.

Another favorite of mine is Peter Tosh. Listening to either of these Jamaican men energizes the fight in me to never stop.

"Emancipate yourselves from mental slavery. None but ourselves can free our minds."

Bob Marley

Goalcast

"How long shall they kill our prophets

While we stand aside and look?"

Redemption Song

Song by Bob Marley

"Consciousness is illegal in the world of fantasy and illusion"
- #Peter Tosh

Right next to foundational Black Americans, no one else has been more vocal about freedom for everyone than the Jamaican culture.

With Jamacia being a top world destination vacation spot like Mexico, of course, I have visited and fallen in love with the intense energy you can feel everywhere—the warrior spirit.

Thank you for these wonderful gifts, Jamacia, and on behalf of Jamaicans to everyone – YOU'RE WELCOME.

One Jamaican man I met told me this story. He said he was born and raised in Jamacia but came to the United States for college.

He says he was in the club one night and had to go to the bathroom.

While in the bathroom, he got into an altercation with a white man.

The police were called.

He says he was thrown in jail without the cops even listening to his side of the story, going totally on what the white man claimed had happened.

He says he was not the aggressor and was released the next day with all charges dropped.

He was appalled, but me knowing America like I know it, I wasn't surprised at all, as this has happened to me as well. I have been thrown in jail for a day or 2 from "trumped-up" charges because the cop just wanted to "show me a lesson on who is in charge."

So, I kind of laughed at his anger and asked him- so that kind of thing couldn't happen to you in Jamacia?

And he said, "No, I am a King here."

"In Jamaica I feel like a human being."
— DR. MARTIN LUTHER KING JR., JUNE 20, 1965, JAMAICA

As you can see, I love Jamaican and Mexican culture very much—one thing I love about both cultures is how proud they are of their country, flag, and bloodline.

I truly hope that love is returned to my culture: Foundational native Black America.

Africa

I would be truly remised if I were to not mention a black continent. I have never been yet but hear time and time again of how beautiful, warm, and vast it is- so I can't wait to visit.

The struggles of this continent are always in my prayers, and I am forever grateful for the many jewels and minerals it provides to the world at a very high cost to its people.

I have loved the vibrancy and directness of most Africans I have met. I am a foundational black American, and we are generally loving people, and I should hope that sentiment is reciprocal.

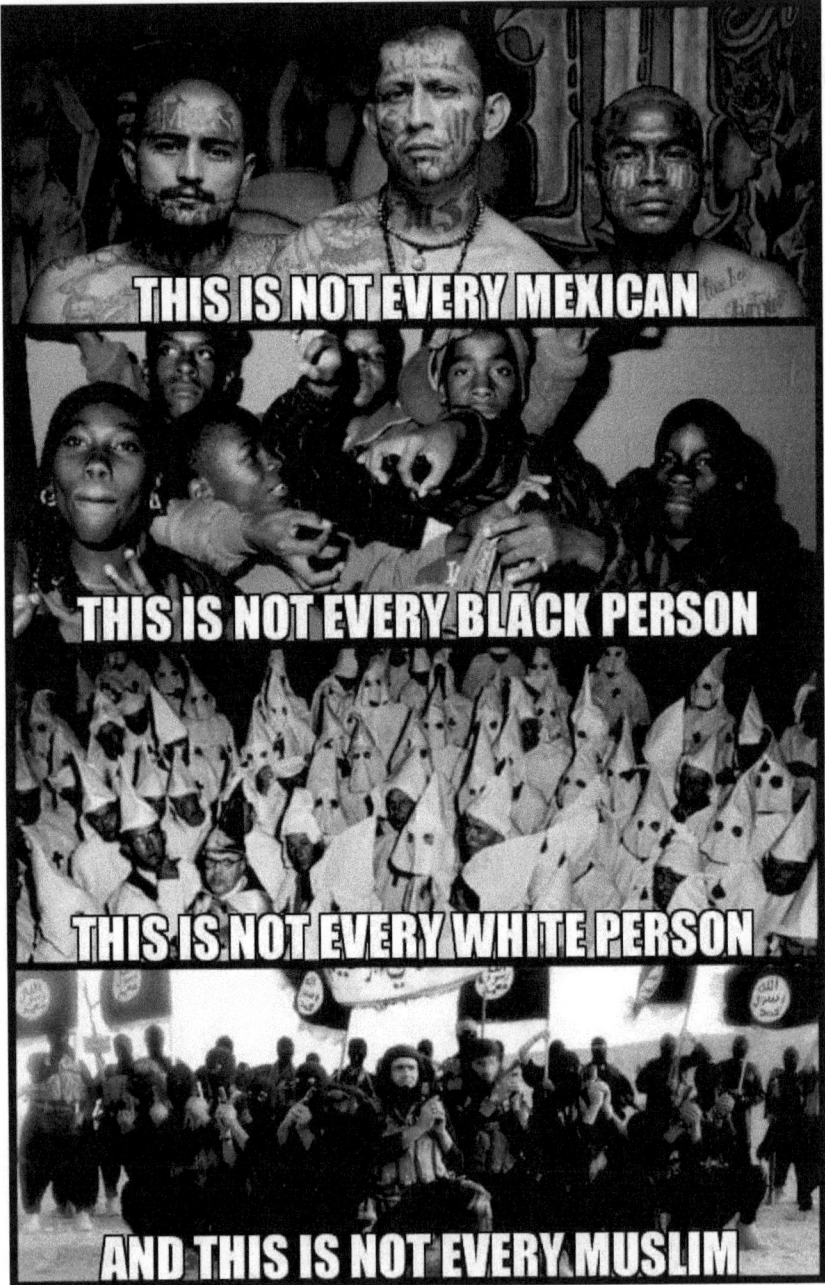

In conclusion

Immigrants and everyone human in general, please forgive me if I am not more versed in your particular culture and background, but as you can see, I have been dealing with more than my fair share here in my own homeland, in America that we all enjoy.

America is truly the land of the brave and home of the free, please come here with that spirit, or you are undermining all the human suffering that took place to make us the greatest country on earth.

Side note: if you hate America, just leave. You are free to go; that's the beauty of America, my country.

No one is tying your hands to stay; please leave. As this is my homeland, I do not want anybody here that does not want to be here.

America is the furthest thing from perfect, but it still is the best thing going. If you think there is somewhere better for you, please go.

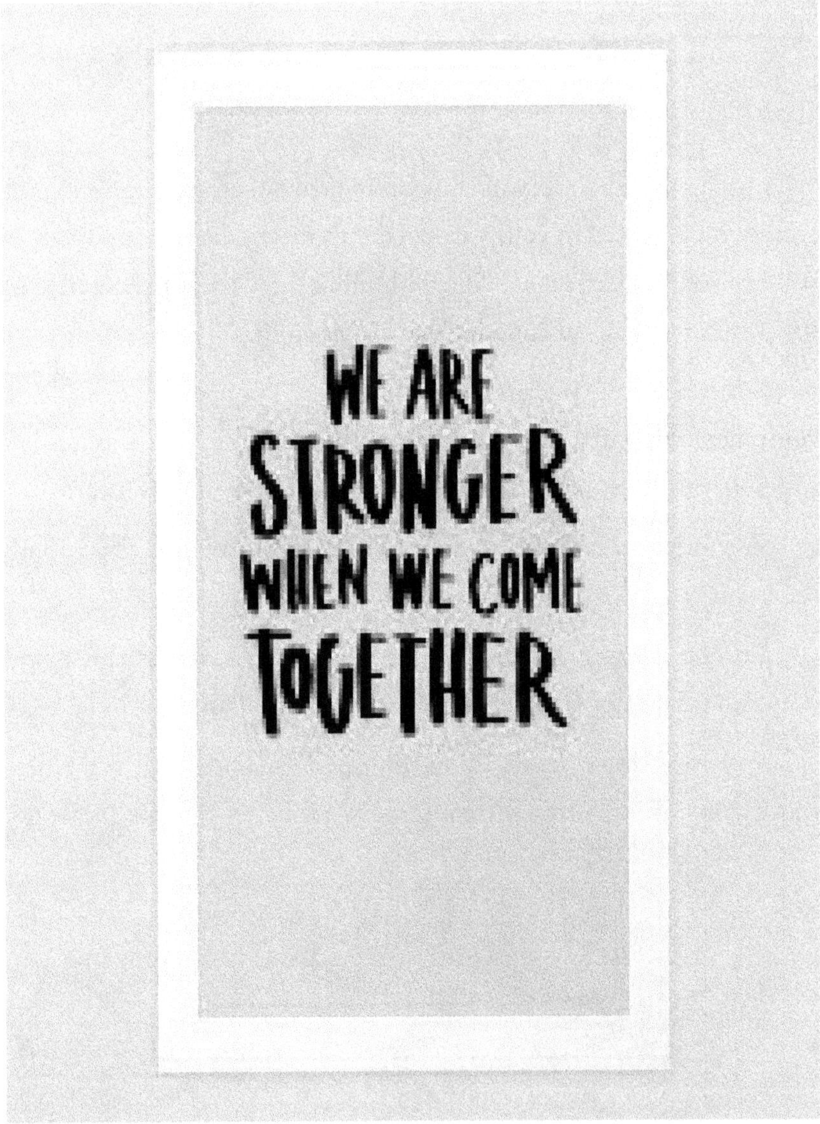
WE ARE
STRONGER
WHEN WE COME
TOGETHER

There should have never been or should never be a color war; it's always about the have and the have nots. But we have been bamboozled into fighting with each other; thus, only making the enemy stronger...tisk, tisk...anywho...once again, this is about love, pride, and admiration for MINE.

The respect and love must be reciprocal, especially on my land.

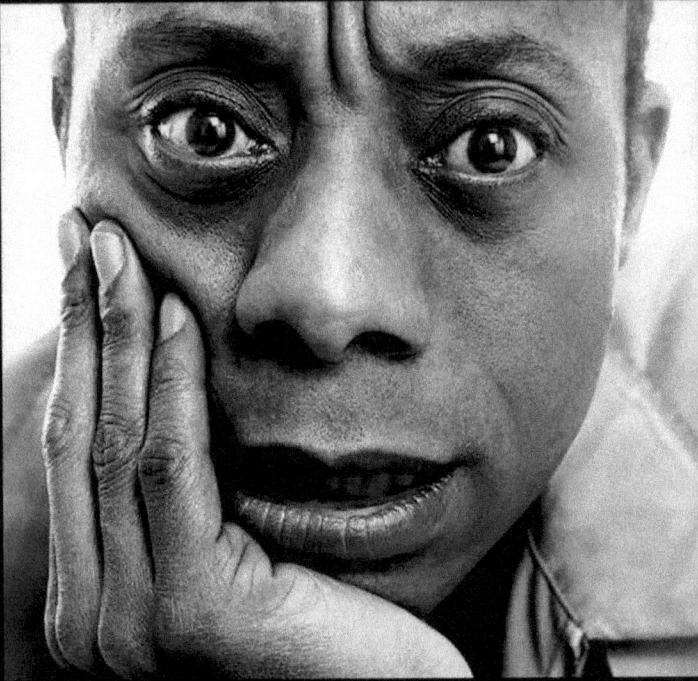

"We can disagree and still love each other... unless your disagreement is rooted in my oppression and denial of my humanity and right to exist."

—James Baldwin

JOIN US ON FACEBOOK AT HUMAN REFORM POLITICS

Stolen Inheritance

Q: Why should I pay for reparations? My family didn't even own slaves. What does this have to do with me?

A: All of us who live in this country, even if our families didn't own slaves, even if we are recent immigrants, have benefited from the 250 years that enslaved people were forced to work without pay. **The American economy was built on the backs of enslaved people,** and neither they nor their ancestors were ever compensated for it. Even after emancipation, formerly enslaved people and their descendants faced unimaginable violence, discrimination, and inequity that has been passed from one generation to the next. Our country's racist criminal justice system and huge racial wealth gap show that white Americans, for the most part unwittingly, continue to reap the benefits of slavery and its legacy.

Q: But wait, didn't we already pay reparations to enslaved people, after the Civil War?

Reparations or boycott

REPARATIONS

How many of you knew that the U.N. was calling for #Reparations for the descendants of Slaves in the United States in 2009? How many of you know that President Obama BOYCOTTED that conference and REFUSED to attend nor discuss the subject? How many of you know that a large part of his refusal was because he felt that they were disrespecting Israel and the Jew-ish community? So he was so intent on standing up for Israel, that he boycotted the conference and cost Black citizens reparations. And not only did he Boycott them, he threatened to cut off relations and trade with any U.S. ally country that attended. So you can ignore the Blacks and 400 years of Slavery & Jim Crow, but you better not offend the Jews on his watch!

MUST INCLUDE
FREE & SEPARATE "LAND" !

Reparations is not Black people wanting something for nothing, instead it is Blacks being fixed because we have been robbed of everything.

We should all be fighting to right America's wrongs.

It's the proverbial elephant in the room.

The playing field has never been leveled for us and we come from a very different starting line.

We are OWED.

As a Foundational Black American, my inheritance has been stolen, and I refuse to let what my great-great-grandmothers and grandfathers went through be in vain.

My Daddy

A Black man, a beautiful human with a magnetic soulful spirit that was undeniable.

A Foundational Black American man who has given his very soul to America. NOONE has paid a higher price to build America than Native Black Americans.

The Foundational Black American man has survived 400 years with a target (literally) square on his back to build this very country the whole world wants to come and enjoy.

Even though my daddy served in the Vietnam war, most of the world would have considered him a "Gangster," but I saw a side to him that most other people probably never had, and that was a glimmer of peace and happiness that we shared in our father/ daughter relationship.

How was America Built??

Off the backs, STRONG BACKS of my ancestors

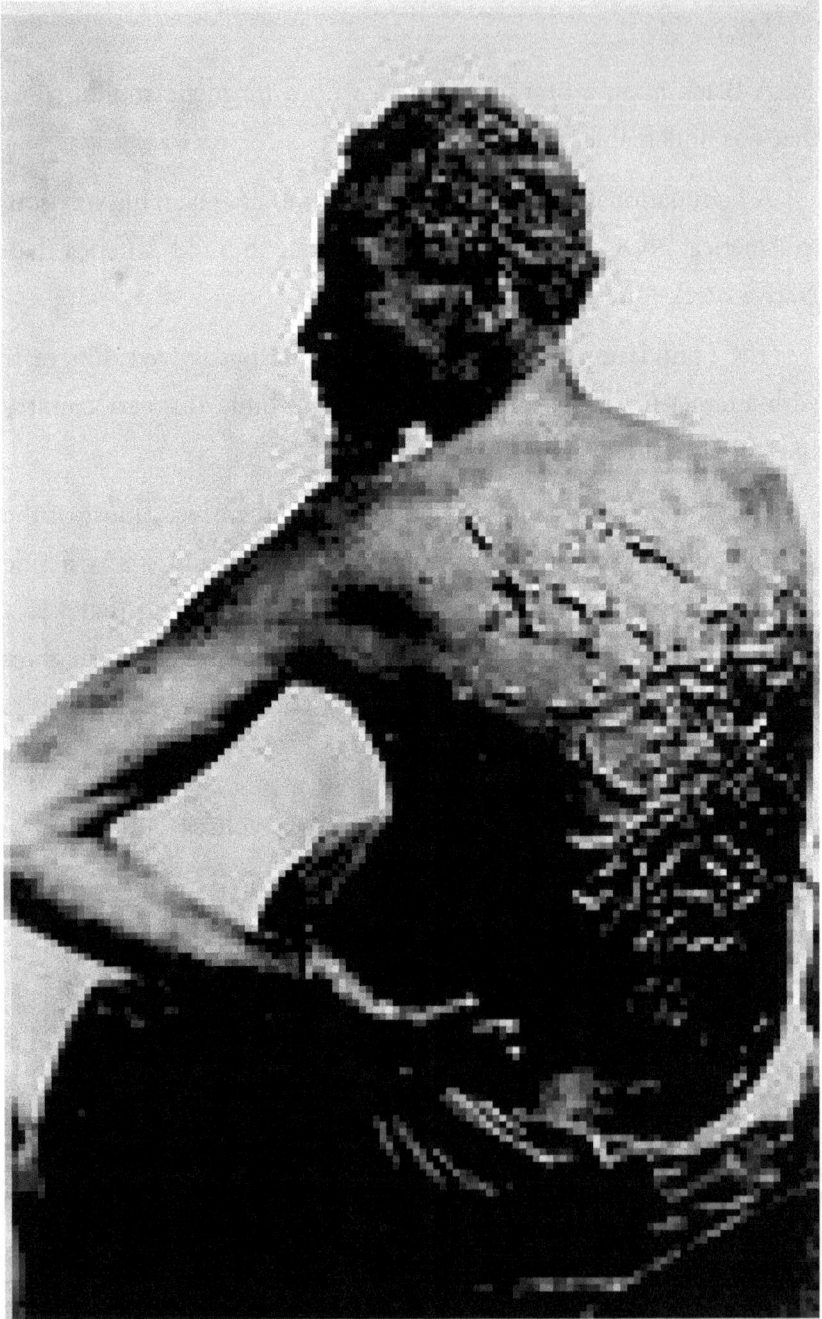

Dont say my name
@stillnez216

Divestors do shit like compare Black men in America to other groups of men knowing damn well the circumstances of Black men in America are unique. No other group has experienced what we have experienced and continue to experience.

But yet we're still here and still achieving.

We were a FUGITIVE or a SLAVE!

When I see pictures of my ancestors, I always think of my daddy.

A black man born in America in the 1930s.

What I saw in him is what was left over after all the atrocities and limited choices he faced for just being born a black boy in America.

And still, WE RISE.

I do not like how my people like my grandmother (foundational black Americans) have been portrayed, looked over, left behind, and DISRESPECTED lately or Ever in our own country!

My grandmother is a FOUNDATIONAL Black AMERICAN. She was not African, Asian, Latino, or European; she was AMERICAN.

So, this book is dedicated to and for Foundational Black Americans, my people who built this here country for free.

Show respect

We love everybody.

This book is just a loving and long overdue ode to MINE.

Thank you

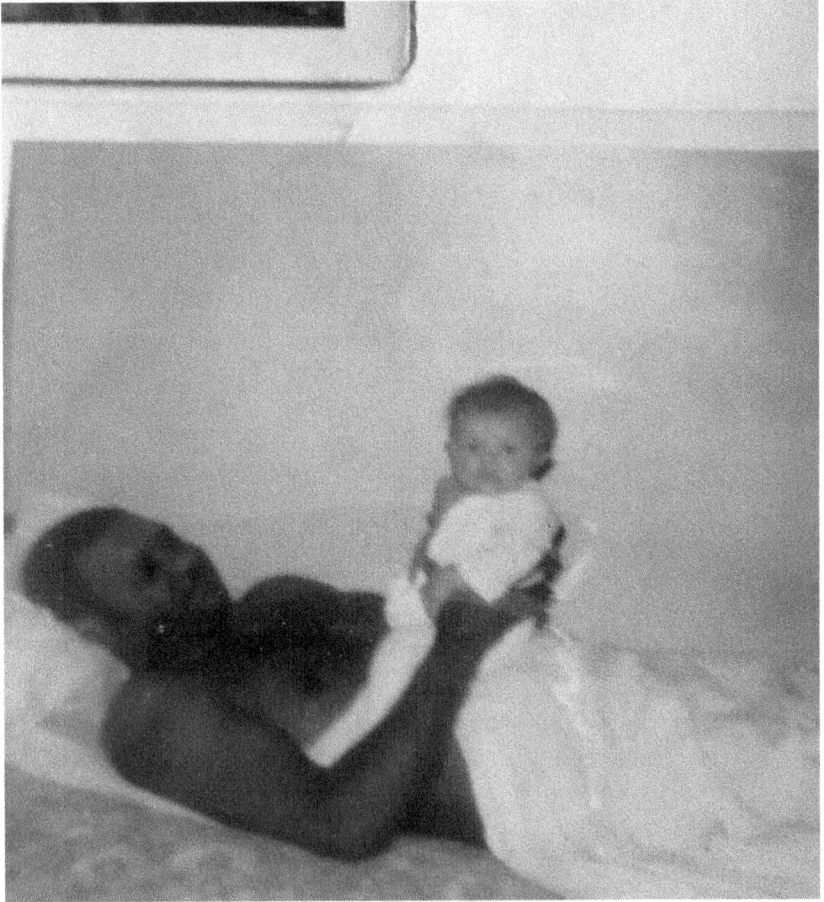

Me and my Daddy

My grandmother, whom I am named after, and myself

Graduating kindergarten with my daddy there.

My uncle Josh and myself

Message to Foundational black native Americans, its's time for us to take care of ourselves while at the same time demanding what our ancestors and now what we are owed. We stand on the shoulders of greatness and have literal superhero DNA in our blood!

The American dollar is the most respected currency in the world – We did that – my ancestors.

The coolest muthafunkers on the planet

Foundational Native Black American Ode

We will never forget,

We will not let it be in Vain

Because of the pain and suffering you endured,

The lynching, the beatings, the torture you withstood.

You paved the way for what we've become today.

From world leaders, activists, and campaigners,

You pushed through and fought to save us.

We wear our rightful crown, with regality, because of your sacrifices

We will never forget,

We will not let it be in Vain

We're pioneers, teachers, leaders, engineers, executives, and peers.

Your legacy is clear; your impact remains strong and without fear.

Thank you, Native black America, for the foundations you laid. And
for enriching our history to this very day.

The dead cannot cry out for justice. It is a duty of the living to do so for them.
Lois McMaster Bujold // Quoteistan.com

Bibliography

History.com Editors. "Jim Crow Laws." *History.com*, A&E Television Networks, 28 Feb. 2018, https://www.history.com/topics/early-20th-century-us/jim-crow-laws.

Restavek Freedom. 2021. *5 American Abolitionists Who Fought to End Slavery - Restavek Freedom*. [online] Available at: <https://restavekfreedom.org/2016/02/25/5-american-abolitionists-who-fought-to-end-slavery/> [Accessed 26 November 2021].

Sinclair, J., 2009. *It's all good*. London: Headpress.

Foster, H., 2021. *COINTELPRO [Counterintelligence Program] (1956-1976)* •. [online] Blackpast.org. Available at: <https://www.blackpast.org/african-american-history/cointelpro-1956-1976/> [Accessed 26 November 2021]

John Brown: The First American to Hang for Treason. (2014, February 12). We're History. http://werehistory.org/john-brown/

Melanin Is Life. "29 Important Facts You Should Know about the Black Panther Party." *Melanin Is Life*, https://melaninislife.com/blogs/lifestyle/important-facts-about-the-black-panther-party.

Kenny, S. (2015, June 11). *How black slaves were routinely sold as 'specimens' to ambitious white doctors*. The Conversation. https://theconversation.com/how-black-slaves-were-routinely-sold-as-specimens-to-ambitious-white-doctors-43074

LET US BE THE ANCESTORS OUR DESCENDANTS WILL THANK

WINONA LADUKE

www.ingramcontent.com/pod-product-compliance
Lightning Source LLC
Chambersburg PA
CBHW060306100426
42742CB00011B/1880